THE KNOWLEDGE OF GOD AND THE SERVICE OF GOD ACCORDING TO THE TEACHING OF THE REFORMATION

THE KNOWLEDGE OF GOD AND THE SERVICE OF GOD ACCORDING TO THE TEACHING OF THE REFORMATION

RECALLING THE SCOTTISH CONFESSION OF 1560

THE GIFFORD LECTURES
DELIVERED IN THE UNIVERSITY OF ABERDEEN
IN 1937 AND 1938

BY

KARL BARTH

TRANSLATED BY

J. L. M. HAIRE AND IAN HENDERSON

Wipf & Stock
PUBLISHERS
Eugene, Oregon

Wipf and Stock Publishers
199 W 8th Ave, Suite 3
Eugene, OR 97401

The Knowledge of God and the Service Of God According
to the Teaching of the Reformation
Recalling the Scottish Confession of 1560
By Barth, Karl
Copyright©1938 Theologischer Verlag Zurich
ISBN: 1-59752-427-1
Publication date 11/1/2005

Previously published by Hodder and Stoughton, 1938

Copyright©1938 Original German version published by
Theologischer Verlag Zurich

.THE text of the Scots Confession which is printed at the beginning of each chapter is that given by P. Schaff in his *Creeds of the Evangelical Protestant Churches*. It is based on the text in Sir John Skene's *Acts of the Parliament of Scotland, 1424–1597*, and has been re-issued recently, along with the Latin Version and an introduction, by Prof. G. D. Henderson of Aberdeen (Church of Scotland Publications).

We wish to draw the reader's attention to the fact that we have rendered " Gottesdienst " throughout by " service " (of God). Occasionally, e.g. in Lectures XVII and XVIII, this word might be equally well or even better translated by " worship " or " public worship ".

We should like to express our thanks to Mr. R. J. Fulton, B.A., and to Miss Maud Fulton, M.A., for their valuable help in reading the proofs and preparing an index.

J. L. M. HAIRE.

IAN HENDERSON.

CONTENTS

PART I—THE KNOWLEDGE OF GOD

SYNOPSIS: LECTURES I-XX

PART I: THE KNOWLEDGE OF GOD

LECTURE I

"NATURAL THEOLOGY" AND THE TEACHING OF THE REFORMATION

1. In good faith towards the will of Lord Gifford we have to establish : (1) that when his will speaks of natural theology it means a knowledge which stands at the disposal of man as man and whose object is the truth about God, the world and man ; (2) that his will expects from the lectures of the Gifford foundation a specific advancement and diffusion of " natural theology " thus understood.

2. A reformed theologian commissioned with the delivery of these lectures cannot, as such, i.e. in loyalty towards his own calling, be in a position to do justice to this task in *direct* agreement and fulfilment of the intention of the testator. He can, however, make this task his own *indirectly*. He can, namely, confer on " natural theology " the loyal and · real service of reminding it of its partner in the conversation. If it wishes to achieve its end in the sense used by the testator it has at least to enter into controversy with this partner, in opposition to whom it must make itself known, prove itself and maintain itself as truth—if it is the truth !

3. This partner to the conversation is, however, *the knowledge of God* and the *service of God according to the teaching of the Reformation*. The positive content of the Reformation is the renewal of the church, based upon the revelation of God in Jesus Christ and this means implicitly the negation of all " natural theology." And " natural theology " can only be developed in implicit and explicit negation of the Reformed teaching. This delimitation cannot, however, be the real intention of these lectures. Also it is only by understanding the positive content of the Reformed teaching that the representative of a " natural theology " can make his position

clear to himself. Only so can he realise that he must hence-
forth make known, prove and maintain even better than formerly
the supposed truth of his subject-matter in antithesis to Reformed
teaching and only so can he make clear to himself the extent
to which he must do so.

Assistance shall be afforded him here to enable him to reach
such an understanding.

4. In accordance with the words of Lord Gifford's will the " natural
theology " which is to be advanced and diffused by means
of the Gifford foundation ought first and foremost to serve the
instruction of " the whole population of Scotland." Since
we are prepared to support his undertaking in the way described
above, let us call to mind that instruction in the Reformed
teaching which was at one time imparted to " the whole population of Scotland " in the form of the *Confessio Scotica* com-
posed and ratified in 1560. We shall listen to this as a witness
to, not as a law of, the Reformed teaching. We shall be
acceding to its own request (Preface and Art. 18) if in repeating,
expounding and presenting it we keep not only to its " historical " text and meaning but primarily and decisively to the
Holy Scripture as heard independently, testimony to which the
Confession claims to be and to whose judgement it has declared itself subject.

LECTURE II

(Art. 1*a*)

THE ONE GOD

1. Reformed teaching is the renewal of the prophetic-apostolic
knowledge of God as knowledge of the one and only God.
Beside and apart from God there is indeed His creation but
no other God. No one and nothing is the Lord in the sense
in which He is the Lord. God is not alone, but God alone is
God.

x

2. This knowledge means above all the limiting of the self-assertion of man who participates in it ; whoever and whatever he may be, he will be unable to conceive himself as identical with God and therefore as having mastery over God. Therefore this knowledge signifies further the relativising of all human ideologies, mythologies, philosophies and religions. Whatever their validity within the created world may be, their objects can certainly not be understood as gods. In the last resort they cannot be considered worthy of belief and proper reverence cannot be paid them.

3. The foundation of this knowledge is absolutely and alone God Himself, Who reveals Himself to man by speaking to him as his Lord in Jesus Christ and Who proves Himself to be the One to Whom no one and nothing is to be preferred or even to be compared. The foundation of this knowledge is therefore not the idea of the One (Monotheism), the direct or indirect propelling power of all philosophical, political and religious systems.

4. Between the claim to lordship of (subjective) human self-assertion and the various claims to lordship of the (objective) world there is unending strife but no decision is reached. But a decision is reached when man, placed between all these claims on the one hand and the claim of God's command on the other, must choose God as the One to Whom alone he can entrust and bind himself definitely and completely and Whom alone he can worship. This decision, which becomes an event in faith in Jesus Christ, is the realisation of the knowledge of the one God. The power to reach this knowledge is the power of God Himself, Who makes it necessary and effective as a decision.

LECTURE III

(Art. 1*b*)

THE GOD OF MAJESTY, THE PERSONAL GOD

1. Who is God ?   Reformed teaching in principle does not answer this question by any free thought, i.e. as if the question had been raised and had to be answered by man himself.   On the contrary, it answers it on the basis of God's own revelation.   That is, it answers it from the standpoint of man who has been told by God Himself in the Person of Jesus Christ who God is, and who has now to render an account to God, and not to himself, for what he has heard from God and has only so to render account to men also.

2. Because Reformed teaching answers God's revelation, it necessarily gives a very humble and a very courageous answer.   It is only in His revelation as Father, Son and Holy Spirit that God has encountered man as the Lord whose freedom and power have neither beginning nor end and who therefore is and remains *hidden* from us in a way in which the most radical scepticism cannot even imagine.   But it is in His revelation as the Lord of Majesty that God, the Father, Son and Holy Spirit has given Himself to be one with man and has therefore made Himself *known* in a way in which even the greatest speculative optimism is in principle superseded.

3. Because the One God is according to His revelation the Father, the Son and the Holy Spirit, He attests His Personality as personality in a *majestic*, pre-eminent sense of the concept, one which is not to be understood in the light of any view of human personality.   God is a free subject, free as the One Who has, does and will establish Himself as a subject in His existence and essence and He is free as the One Who has absolute mastery over His own existence and essence and similarly through these has absolute mastery over all other existence and essence.

xii

Thus God is *majestic* just because He is personal, and hidden just because He declares His name : I am—*that I am.* He is *incomprehensibly* personal.

4. Because the One God is according to His revelation the Father, the Son and the Holy Spirit, He attests His majesty in a *personal* and therefore concrete sense of the term, a sense which is not to be understood in the light of any human idea of the " Absolute." He is neither nothing, nor is He all, nor is He the one in all. *His* majesty consists in His being the archetype of what we ourselves are, i.e. He is the One, He it is Who knows, wills, acts and speaks ; in His complete freedom He is " *I* " in Himself, " *Thou* " and " *He* " for us. Thus God is *personal* just because He is majestic and He declares His true name just because He remains hidden to us : *I am*—that I am. He is *incomprehensibly* majestic.

LECTURE IV

(Art. 1c-2b)

THE GLORY OF GOD AND THE GLORY OF MAN

1. According to Reformed teaching, alongside the glory of God and for His glory, the world created by Him and man in particular have also a glory peculiar to them, i.e. a truth, an independence, a significance, a dignity and an appointed destiny of their own. The order in which they stand is of course that the glory of the world and man as one bestowed upon them by God for His own glory, is established by God's glory alone and is completely conditioned and bound to it.

2. Because God reveals Himself to man in Jesus Christ, it is established firstly that not only does God Himself *exist* but that from God, by Him and for Him there *exists* also a real world and man in particular, which is distinct from Him. God does not rest satisfied with the fullness of the glory which He possesses

xiii

in Himself but the glory which He possesses in Himself overflows in His making it the peculiar and perfect glory of the world created by Him and of man in particular to serve His own glory and in His being therefore Creator and Lord of this world and of man, without standing in need of them, in virtue of His eternal love.

3. Because God reveals Himself to man in Jesus Christ, it is established secondly that the existence of the world and of man in particular is grace, i.e. that it has its glory in the overflowing glory of God and not in itself and hence neither in its spiritual nor in its natural side, neither in its coming into being nor in its passing away, neither in its freedom nor in its necessity. Its being permitted to be gratitude for God's grace and to serve His glory is what makes it true and real and possessed of meaning and purpose.

4. Because God reveals Himself to man in Jesus Christ it is established thirdly that in the midst of the real world in its entirety it is man who is called to be thankful, i.e. to recognise God's glory in his own existence and to actualise it and in doing so to trust God who is Creator and Lord of the rest of the world besides.

5. The points which we have established are not a matter of abstract conjecture and reflection about " God," the " World " and " Man," but a matter of the exposition of the concrete revelation given in the Person of Jesus Christ. In this God Himself has confirmed and explained the order of the relation between His glory and the glory of man described above.

LECTURE V

(Art. 2c-3)

THE WAY OF MAN

1. The way of man as the way he goes *himself* is the history of his attempt to seize the glory of God for himself and is, therefore, necessarily the history of the loss of his own glory. The way

of man, however, as the way in which *God* goes with him is the history of Jesus Christ, i.e. the history of the victory in which God proves His glory even in the Fall of man and is therefore necessarily the history of the restoration of man's glory also.

2. By revealing Himself to man in Jesus Christ, God brings against man the accusation that his *own* way is the way of ingratitude towards God's grace. Man, unfaithful to his calling, which is to serve God's glory, makes himself the lord of his life, as if he were God. What he *does* thereby, he would have to *be*, without prospect of deliverance, if God withdrew His hand from him, viz. deprived of his own glory, i.e. a prisoner to the contradiction of his own nature, lost in a world which has ceased to have a lord and therefore ceased to have a meaning for him and subject to vanity. Man's own way is the way of sin, i.e. of offence against God, which only God can make amends for.

3. By revealing Himself to man in Jesus Christ, God gives him the promise and commands him to believe, that it is He, God Himself, who makes amends for the evil done by man. This, man's own way, is also the way in which God goes with him by becoming man in Jesus Christ. It is the way in which He confers on him the new unmerited glory of calling him His child, a glory which cannot be destroyed by any debt or punishment.

4. A pessimistic anthropology has nothing to do with that accusation and an optimistic anthropology has nothing to do with that promise. It is the Holy Spirit of God Himself who humiliates man as sinner, exalts him as believer and who enables him to be recognised in this humiliation and exaltation.

LECTURE VI

(Art. 4-6)

THE REVELATION OF GOD IN JESUS CHRIST

1. The revelation of God in Jesus Christ is the history of God's faithfulness in the midst of man's unfaithfulness and is therefore the history of the way of the grace of God with sinful man. In the testimony of the Old Testament the revelation of God is the history of the church which lives by the promise of Jesus Christ. In the testimony of the New Testament it is the history of Jesus Christ Himself. This twofold and inseparable history is at once the source and the subject of the Reformed teaching.

2. To instruct the church about herself, the revelation of God is borne witness to in the Old Testament as the history of a people, which, as a sinful people, has been elected and called, sustained and increased, blessed and led by God. Although it does not possess more than the promise and the command to have faith and although it ends its history in confirming man's unfaithfulness by the rejection of Jesus Christ, nevertheless by its existence it testifies to the fact that the promise given to it has a ground and the faith commanded it has an object.

3. To instruct the church about her Lord and Saviour, the revelation of God is borne witness to in the New Testament as the history of Jesus Christ, Who as true Son of God has assumed true manhood and Who, rejected by men but confirming God's faithfulness, has thereby reconciled sinful man with God in His own person. In the humiliation of His divine nature and in the exaltation of His human nature He is the goal, the significance and the content of the history of that people, the ground of its promise and the object of its faith, the ruling head of its church.

4. The historical and critical study of the Bible performs the task of understanding the human documents of the Old Testament

xvi

and the New Testament as human documents. The question as to their divine content is not a question for critical study as such, but is the question with which faith has to do and is perhaps also the one with which superstition, error and unbelief are concerned.

LECTURE VII

(Art. 7-8)

GOD'S DECISION AND MAN'S ELECTION

1. Jesus Christ in His unity as true God and true man is the eternal, merciful decision of the just God for fellowship with sinful man and thereby the eternal, merciful election of sinful man for fellowship with the just God—a decision and election consummated in time.

2. Jesus Christ is *God's decision* for man. It is free mercy that God decides for man and not against him. But that which for us is mercy is strict justice in the case of Jesus Christ, because He is the true God and because God in His human life and death has *Himself* taken our place and therefore finds His perfection again in the active obedience of this man and so is in pure fellowship with Him.

3. Jesus Christ is *man's election* for God. It is free mercy that man is permitted to live with God and is not compelled to perish without Him. But that which for us is mercy is strict justice in the case of Jesus Christ, because He is true man and because God in His human life and death has Himself taken *our place* and therefore finds *our* guilt atoned for in the suffering and obedience of this man and so is in pure fellowship with Him.

4. God's decision and man's election is not a general truth (either in the sense of a hidden divine decree or in the sense of a quality of discernment belonging to man). It is exclusively the truth of the God-man Jesus Christ which is described above and which can be grasped in faith.

xvii

LECTURE VIII

(Art. 9-10)

GOD'S WORK AND MAN'S SALVATION

1. The salvation of man is his translation out of sin into righteousness before God and out of death into the fullness of life with God. This translation is not his own work but that of God. And this work of God is the death and resurrection of Jesus Christ as the epitome of the Incarnation of the Son of God.

2. Jesus Christ the crucified is *God in His humiliation*, i.e. in His self-sacrifice—in His participation in the curse, the plight and the despair of the existence of sinful man. In this, however, He does not cease to be true God, but He takes—and this is the mystery of the Cross—the sin, guilt and punishment of man away from him and upon Himself. For His sake (in Him alone and in Him once and for all) sin is *forgiven* us for time and eternity.

3. Jesus Christ the risen is *man in His exaltation*, i.e. in His being raised up and transfigured through the power of God, in His participation in God's majesty. In this, however, he does not cease to be true man but He realises—and this is the mystery of the Resurrection—a life of man in eternal righteousness, innocence and blessedness. For His sake (in Him alone and in Him once and for all) this righteousness is *ascribed* to us for time and eternity.

4. Because the salvation of man through God's humiliation and man's exaltation is not our own but God's work, the work of Jesus Christ both crucified and risen, therefore the salvation of man can be brought about neither through the acts of a cult nor through the endeavours of a morality but can only be *received* through faith.

xviii

xix

LECTURE X

(Art. 12)

FREEDOM TO BELIEVE

1. To know God means, according to Reformed teaching, to be a new man who obeys God and therefore believes in Jesus Christ as the prophet, priest and king in whom God Himself has acted, acts and will act.

2. By believing in Jesus Christ and receiving the salvation brought about by Him alone, man recognises his own unfaithfulness and therefore ceases to believe in himself. Therefore he cannot understand his faith as a work which he would be free to do by means of his own strength, for which he would possess in his own powers the organ and the capacity, and which he could prepare for, start, persevere in or continue by his own skill and achievements.

3. By believing in Jesus Christ and receiving the salvation brought about by Him alone, man recognises God's faithfulness. Therefore he may understand his freedom to believe, i.e. to live a new life in obedience and hope, as the wonderful and unmerited but real gift of the Holy Spirit. According to Reformed teaching it is God alone through whom God is recognised in truth by sinful man reconciled through Him.

PART II: THE SERVICE OF GOD

LECTURE XI

(Art. 13)

THE REAL CHRISTIAN LIFE

1. The essence of all good action consists in the renewing of man through the Holy Spirit, and therefore through faith in Jesus Christ (cf. Lecture 10). This renewing is what makes the Christian life real and is as such the meaning of the span of life alloted to man.

2. Since man knows in faith the God who in Jesus Christ graciously intervenes on his behalf, he knows that he himself is God's enemy and therefore a sinner, but also knows that he is acquitted of this sin and really separated from it. He knows his sin as that element of his existence which is alien to himself. He acknowledges that it has happened, is happening and will happen. But he can own allegiance to it no longer and he may own allegiance to the grace which forgives it.

3. Faith means the divine crisis which overtakes human existence, in the course of which man is convicted again and again of his sin, but is also and to a much greater extent assured again and again of God's grace, in order that he may give God the glory in all the decisions in which both conviction of sin and assurance of grace become actual every day.

4. The real Christian life consists therefore in the accomplishment of daily thankfulness and repentance which, when it is efficacious and genuine, is not the good or bad fruit of our efforts, but is as a reiteration of faith in Jesus Christ the work of the Holy Spirit.

LECTURE XII

(Art. 14)

THE ORDINANCE GOVERNING THE CHRISTIAN LIFE

1. The ordinance governing the Christian Life is the Divine Law. Man has not himself to decide about what is good or evil, or about what is enjoined or forbidden. God has decided about that by His having given to His grace, revealed in Jesus Christ, the form of a definite claim upon man, and by His having therefore given to faith in Jesus Christ the form of definite obedience.

2. Jesus Christ has come to us as true God, that as such He might *perfectly* take our place and make us partakers of eternal life (cf. Lectures 7 and 8). Therefore the Divine Law demands

xxi

that man, because he believes in Jesus Christ, should honour and call upon *God*, attend to His Word, seek Him in the ways which He Himself has shown man, and receive His salvation through the means which He Himself has given man.

3. Jesus Christ has come to us as true man, that as such He might really take *our place* and so partake of the misery and despair of sinful man (*cf.* Lectures 7 and 8). Therefore the Divine Law demands that man, because he believes in Jesus Christ, should exist for his *fellow men*, and render them as limited and weak human beings, honour, service and help.

4. The ordinance governing the Christian life, the way of thankfulness and repentance, the criterion of good and evil is therefore faith in Jesus Christ, which as such cannot exist without love to God and man and thus without the fulfilment of the true, the Divine Law.

LECTURE XIII

(Art. 15)

THE TRUE CHRISTIAN LIFE

1. Our thankfulness and our repentance are true obedience and are acknowledged by God as fulfilment of His Law, in so far as they are the work of faith in Jesus Christ, active in love, and therefore in so far as Jesus Christ intervenes on our behalf by His suffering and obedience. He and He alone is the true Christian life.

2. Precisely because Jesus Christ intervenes on our behalf by His suffering and obedience, we, regardless of the actual insincerity, superficiality and imperfection of our outward and inward achievement, are and remain in all circumstances and without intermission claimed for obedience to God's Law and therefore for Christian life in love for God and man.

3. Precisely because Jesus Christ intervenes on our behalf by His suffering and obedience, we, regardless of the actual sincerity, depth and perfection of our outward and inward achievement,

are and remain dependent on the sin-forgiving grace of God, and are therefore without the possibility of pleading before God our Christian life as our own glory and merit or of basing our confidence on any kind of reference to our own achievement

LECTURE XIV

(Art. 16-17, 25a)

THE MYSTERY OF THE CHURCH

1. The Christian life is the life of the church of Jesus Christ hidden in God and manifest to men. That is to say (cf. Lecture 6), it is the life of the people, which through Jesus Christ has been gathered to be one in Him, in spite of all the diversity of the individuals thus brought together, of their position in time and of the limitations of the age to which they belong, and which has been elected and called to holiness in Him in spite of all human sinfulness. This people consists of those who in faith in Jesus Christ are reconciled to God, and who, because thus reconciled, may proclaim the glory of God.

2. Jesus Christ is never without His people, but in the humiliation of His divine nature and the exaltation of His human nature is always the goal, the meaning and the content of its history, the ground of the promise to, and the object of the faith of this, His people. Because of this, there is no reconciliation of man, and therefore no Christian life outside the church. The faith, active in love, of the individual man is not his own private concern, but consists in his participation in the hidden and manifest life of the body whose head is Jesus Christ.

3. The mystery of the church and of our participation in her life is the divine hiddenness of the work of the Holy Spirit, through which individual men are called to faith, active in love, and so to Christian life, and thus to life in the church.

4. Whether our participation in the life of the church as manifested to men means that we are also partakers in her life hidden in God, is something which must be decided again and again in

the actualisation of faith. But there can be no participation in the life of the church hidden in God which would not also mean immediately and directly our participation in her life as manifested to men.

LECTURE XV

(Art. 18*a*)

THE FORM OF THE CHURCH

1. The one universal and holy church of Jesus Christ exists, as manifested to men, in the form of individual churches, which , differ in time and place, but which in Jesus Christ as their head, and therefore in their faith and work, are uniformly determined.

2. The existence of the church as manifested to men as individual churches involves a distinction which has to be drawn over and over again in the history of these individual churches, the distinction, namely, between the true and the false church, that is, between the church founded, sustained and ordered by Jesus Christ and that set up, defended and made use of by men on their own authority.

3. The existence of the true church of Jesus Christ in an individual church (or the existence of an individual church as the true church ot Jesus Christ) stands or falls with the work of the Holy Spirit taking place within this individual church. The question as to the true church can never be decided anywhere by means of the standards which we as human beings have at our disposal.

4. But the spiritual distinction between the true church and the false is carried into effect and made manifest in so far as the life of each individual church is *reformed*, that is, as in accordance with faith, active in love it is made subject to the Word of God as the Revelation of His Grace in Jesus Christ.

SYNOPSIS

LECTURE XVI

(Art. 18b-20)

THE GOVERNMENT OF THE CHURCH

1. The church cannot be governed either by the majority of its
   members or by a special ecclesiastical order—in no sense can
   she be governed by herself but only by the Word of God, by
   which she also has been founded and is sustained. But the
   Word of God is Holy Scripture, i.e. the testimony of the
   prophets and apostles to the revelation of God in Jesus Christ.
   Because it is by the voice of the Holy Spirit alone that the true
   church is both created and distinguished from the false church,
   she cannot listen to the voice of a stranger alongside His.
2. The church cannot therefore understand her course as a history
   of arbitrary human opinions and resolutions. She understands
   it rather as the exposition of Holy Scripture by itself, as the
   Word of God acting in her. Human opinions and resolutions
   can never precede but only follow the decisions of the Word
   of God and the church can never have the truth of the Word
   of God at her disposal but can only be its servant.
3. If the church on her side makes definite decisions, she does so
   because she must constantly justify her actions before the
   Word of God which governs her, and must constantly profess
   the truth in the face of error. The bonds she thus imposes
   can and will provide not a hindrance but rather free course to
   the Word of God. They are valid and effective in so far as
   the church in them owes allegiance not to herself but to Jesus
   Christ as her head and thus to Holy Scripture.
4. Provided that Holy Scripture alone governs the church, the valid
   constitution of government can in itself be built up equally
   well on the basis of an ecclesiastical order or on the basis of
   the congregation. But the freedom of the Word of God is
   better served and hence so also is the legitimate authority of
   the bonds necessarily imposed if the congregation is and remains in itself the bearer of the church's responsibility towards
   the Word of God.

LECTURE XVII

(Art. 21)

THE CHURCH SERVICE AS DIVINE ACTION

1. The primary *ground* of the church service is neither devotional nor instructional. Nor is it the confession made by the human beings who take part in it, but the presence and action of Jesus Christ Himself and hence the work of the divine creation and sustaining of the church and of the Christian life of her members—a work which is the meaning and goal of all human history.

2. The primary *content* of the church service is therefore the work of the Holy Spirit both in the proclamation of the revelation of God in Jesus Christ, determined and delimited by baptism and the Lord's Supper, and in the faith which is established and nourished by this proclamation—a faith in which man, in spite of his natural lack of faith and disobedience, commits himself to the gracious and almighty lordship and care of God.

3. The primary *form* of the church service is given with that proclamation's human means and signs which are instituted through the revelation of God in Jesus Christ. This, the form of the church service, cannot be confounded with its content and hence cannot be made absolute, as if Jesus Christ had rendered Himself superfluous through the human institution of the church. But this, the form of the church service, cannot be detached from its content, and cannot therefore be lightly esteemed and neglected as if Jesus Christ did not wish to glorify Himself expressly in the human institution of the church.

LECTURE XVIII

(Art. 22-23)

THE CHURCH SERVICE AS A HUMAN ACTION

1. The secondary *ground* of the church service is not the religious need or capacity of the human beings who take part in it but the necessity of obedience to the gracious will of Jesus Christ, present and active in their midst—a necessity which unites them into the church. This obedience is also the service which the church owes to the whole world.

2. The secondary *content* of the church service consists therefore in such action on the part of the congregation as has for its goal a new, more loyal and more efficacious hearing of the revelation of God in Jesus Christ and thus the glory of God's name in its own midst and throughout the whole world. In this action both those who belong to the ecclesiastical order and those who belong to the rest of the congregation possess a promise and a responsibility which is in each case their own, yet is in each case of the same importance in the sight of God and in their relation to one another, and in the last resort is common to both.

3. The secondary *form* of the church service consists in an effort which is unceasingly the task of the whole congregation and which must always be repeated anew. It is the effort, critical in spirit, after a sincere and humble proclamation and understanding of the divine Word—a proclamation and understanding which correspond to the institution of the church as originated by Jesus Christ.

LECTURE XIX

(Art. 24)

THE STATE'S SERVICE OF GOD

1. No sphere exists in which Jesus Christ is not already to-day secretly or openly the only Lord and the supreme judge. No other law exists which can have the right of limiting the church's task and of setting aside faith in Jesus Christ, active in love. The political order in its varying forms is no less an order for the service of God, in which rulers and ruled are called to obedience to God, to thankfulness and to penitence.

2. The significance of the political order as service of God is clearly seen, wherever the form of political power then in force honours God by providing for justice and peace, so far as human insight and human ability can, and by providing and preserving freedom for the true church to proclaim the forgiveness of sins and eternal life in accordance with the task laid upon her. The significance of the political order as service of God is obscured, wherever the form of political power then in force seeks to operate for its own advantage, violating and suppressing justice and peace, advancing the false church or becoming itself the false church.

3. Faith in Jesus Christ, active in love, will enter on positive co-operation in the tasks and aims of the political power then in force or it will passively withdraw from this power's responsibility according in either case as the significance of the state as service of God is made clear or obscured in its application by the political power.

4. The duty of obedience to the political order, which is bound up with its significance—made clear or obscured—of serving God, and the duty of prayer for the holders of the form of political power then in force, does not cease, but merely adopts a new form, when a choice must be made in the conflict between faith in Jesus Christ, active in love, and the claims of a particular political power, and when, this being the case, God must be obeyed rather than men.

LECTURE XX

(Art. 25*b*)

THE GIFT OF COMFORT AND HOPE

1. The necessity but also the questionableness and danger of the service rendered by the state to God reminds the church of the fact that her life and all Christian life here and now takes place within the bounds of a still unredeemed world of sinful men, whose reconciliation with God is indeed *already* accomplished in Jesus Christ, yet is *still hidden.*

2. The power with which the church serves her Lord here and now and the confidence with which she does so, cannot therefore be founded on what men can feel and think, say and do within the compass of the church. They find their basis in the comfort given to these men, which tells them that their sins are forgiven in Jesus Christ, and in the certain hope that Jesus Christ Himself, as Lord of all creation, will reveal His righteousness as eternal life.

3. On the basis of this comfort and this hope the confession of the church begins and ends with the *prayer* for that action of the one God, Father, Son and Holy Spirit, which alone makes all human knowledge of God and all human service of God true, and which makes amends for all human error and all human disobedience. It is from the revelation of this Triune God that the church springs and it is the same revelation that she goes to meet.

PART I

THE KNOWLEDGE OF GOD

LECTURE I

"NATURAL THEOLOGY" AND THE TEACHING OF THE REFORMATION

I

Lord Gifford, who died in 1887, left a will containing two unambiguously clear requirements in regard to the lectures to be held in the four Scottish Universities on the basis of the lectureship founded by him. The law of good faith towards the will of the founder demands that those who have the honour to be commissioned with the holding of this lectureship shall take note of these requirements without altering their meaning. It requires also that the content of their lectures shall meet these requirements within the limits of what is possible for the lecturers. The two requirements of Lord Gifford are as follows :—

1. The lecturers shall have as their subject " Natural Theology " " in the widest sense of the term " ; by this is clearly meant the highest perfection of what in the history of the Christian church has generally been understood by " Natural Theology "—a science of God, of the relations in which the world stands to Him and of the human ethics and morality resulting from the knowledge of Him. This science is to be constructed independently of all historical religions and religious bodies as a strict natural science like chemistry and astronomy " without reference to or reliance upon any supposed special exceptional or so-called miraculous revelation." According to the presuppositions of " Natural Theology " as Lord Gifford

understood the term—and he was perfectly correct in understanding it in this way—there does exist a knowledge of God and His connection with the world and men, apart from any special and supernatural revelation. This is a knowledge which perhaps requires and is capable of development and cultivation, but is none the less a knowledge which man as man is master of, just as he is of chemical and astronomical knowledge. It is a knowledge of which man, since as man he still stands in an original relation to God, indisputably possesses, and it is therefore a knowledge which he only requires to discover, as something which he himself possesses, as he discovers the mathematical laws which lie at the basis of chemistry and astronomy, in order then to apply them to these sciences. It is just this knowledge which is at man's disposal from his origin, which " Natural Theology " has in the course of its development to present.

2. The Gifford Lectures shall serve the " promoting, advancing, teaching and diffusing " of the study of such natural theology, and that " among all classes of society " and " among the whole population of Scotland." What is required therefore is both a definite service *intensively*, the deepening and clarifying of this science within itself, to be afforded by means of these lectures, and a definite service *extensively*—public teaching in its import and propaganda for its methods and results.

II

I feel that more than one, though perhaps not all, of those who in the past have given these lectures must have had to rack their brains over these require= ments of Lord Gifford's, but I am sure that to none of my distinguished predecessors have they given so much trouble as to me.

Permit me to state at once quite frankly the reason for this. I certainly see—with astonishment—that such a science as Lord Gifford had in mind does exist, but I do not see how it is possible for it to exist. I am convinced that so far as it has existed and still exists, it owes its existence to a radical error. How then should I be in a position to further and to spread it ? Further, the difficulty with which I am faced, so far as I understand the matter, does not lie merely in the personal opinions which I happen to possess. It lies in a circumstance much more important and compelling than any private opinion—namely, in my calling as a theologian of the Reformed Church, a calling which I cannot well exchange for any other, e.g. for that of a philosopher or psychologist. If I wish to remain in my calling and true to it—and I have no choice in the matter—I am not in the position to do justice to the task set me by Lord Gifford's will " in *direct* affirmation and fufilment of the in- tention of the testator." As a Reformed theologian I am subject to an ordinance which would keep me away from " Natural Theology," even if my personal opinions inclined me to it. I am of course aware that both in the past and in recent times there have been Reformed theologians also, to whom " Natural Theology," at least in a rather weakened and obscure sense of the term, appeared to be no impossible pursuit. I feel, however, that precisely the strong and clear sense in which this conception appears in the will of Lord Gifford, must make it clear even to the most innocent of men—even if he does not know it otherwise—that it cannot really be the business of a Reformed theologian to raise so much as his little finger to support this undertaking in any positive way.

In the face of this critical state of affairs I am happy to be in a position to mention that in the summer of 1935, after I had received the honour of being invited to give these lectures, I expressly reminded the Senatus of this University of the fact that " I am an avowed opponent of all natural theology." Since this invitation was none the less sustained and a part of the responsibility for the resulting situation has been taken from me, I would like briefly to explain in what sense I propose to bear my share of this responsibility and to satisfy the duty of good faith toward the will of the testator, since I have accepted this invitation.

I do not know anything which could prevent me from doing justice at least *indirectly* to his intentions. " Natural Theology " is thrown into relief by the dark *background* of a totally different theology. It is openly or secretly conducting a *discussion* with this other theology. It exists in *antithesis* to this theology and, as the will of Lord Gifford itself clearly shows, it has its whole *emotional appeal* in its antithesis to this other theology. " Natural Theology " has to make itself known, demonstrate itself and maintain itself over against this other theology by distinguishing itself from it and protesting against it. How could it do otherwise ? It has at any rate never done otherwise with vigour and success. When " Natural

Theology " has this opponent no longer in view, it is notorious how soon it tends to become arid and listless. And when its conflict with this adversary no longer attracts attention, it is also notorious that interest too in " Natural Theology " soon tends to flag. Why then should the service not be rendered it of presenting to it once more this its indispensable opponent, since the requirement is that " Natural Theology " shall here be served ? And this opponent is that totally different theology by which " Natural Theology " lives, in so far as it must affirm what the other denies and deny what the other affirms. I could well imagine that there could be nothing more animating and stimulating for all wholehearted and halfhearted friends of " Natural Theology " than to listen to this totally different theology once again. I could well imagine that by gaining a hearing for the voice of this totally different theology, to the best of my ability and understanding, I may actually win new friends and new sympathy for " Natural Theology " in all spheres of society. I could well imagine that all those who do not know that ordinance which prevents me from devoting myself to " Natural The- ology " will, on hearing my lectures, feel themselves confirmed in their intention to devote themselves for their part all the more to " Natural Theology." But however that may be, it can only be to the good of " Natural Theology " to be able once again to measure itself as the truth—if it is the truth !—by that which from its point of view is the greatest of errors. Oppor- tunity is to be given it to do this here. And in this sense I propose to satisfy Lord Gifford's requirements.

III

This background and antithesis to " Natural The-ology," however, is *the knowledge of God and the service of God according to the teaching of the Reformation*, and it is about this that I would like to speak in these lectures, all the time continuing in my calling and subject to its ordinance, and continuing true to both of them. Roman Catholic theology stands in no clear antithesis to " Natural Theology " and just as little does this antithesis hold good of modern Protestant theology, as it has attained sway in most non-Roman churches since about the year 1700. Both are based on compromises with " Natural Theology." Were I a Roman Catholic or a Protestant Modernist, I could not render " Natural Theology " the service which I would like to render it here. But the Reformation and the teaching of the Reformation churches stand in an antithesis to " Natural Theology " which is at once clear and instructive for both.

It is well known that the sixteenth century was not yet able to see that so clearly as we must see it to-day after the developments of the last four hundred years. The Reformers occasionally made a guarded and con-ditional use of the possibility of " Natural Theology" (as, e.g. Calvin in the first chapters of his Institutes), but they made occasionally also an unguarded and unconditional use of it (as did, e.g. Luther and Calvin in their teaching on the Law)—that, however, in no way alters the principle, that the revival of the gospel by Luther and Calvin consisted in their desire to see both the church and human salvation founded on the

Word of God *alone*, on God's *revelation in Jesus Christ*, as it is attested in the Scripture, and on faith in that Word. This is the reason why their teaching—if we disregard the fact that in its historical form it is not absolutely free from certain elements of " Natural Theology "—is the clear antithesis to that form of teaching which declares that man himself possesses the capacity and the power to inform himself about God, the world and man. From the point of view of Reformed teaching what could be more impossible than this task, undertaken by all " Natural Theology " ? And similarly because the teaching of the Reformation is so absolute an opponent of " Natural Theology," the latter could have no other opponent, whom it must look full in the face so frankly and with so much interest. We shall have opportunity here and there in these lectures to make this antithesis clear.

But the proving of this antithesis is not to be the aim of these lectures. They will not therefore be devoted to the refutation of " Natural Theology." This is not only because this aim would be incompatible with good faith towards Lord Gifford's will. The decisive reason is that the Reformation teaching does not live by its antithesis to " Natural Theology " in the way in which the latter lives by its antithesis to Reformed teaching. Even if there were no " Natural Theology," Reformed teaching would be just as it is. It lives independently by its positive content. For this reason we must turn our attention to this positive content—and we must do so for the sake of our proposed service to " Natural Theology " as well. If it is to know whom it is contradicting and if it is really to have the opportunity once more of measuring itself by its most dangerous opponent, it must not hear exclusively or even primarily this opponent's denial of it, but must first and foremost hear the positive affirmation of that opponent, in order that then and from that position it may perhaps also understand the denial which is directed against it. In these lectures I shall therefore endeavour to speak not negatively but *positively*, without, however, losing sight of the problem of " Natural Theology."

IV

In order to remind us that we are dealing here not with my personal opinions but with the teaching of the Reformed church, these lectures on that teaching will not take the form of an independent outline, but will be connected with a *document* of the Reformation. Further, taking into account the specifically Scottish character of the Gifford foundation, this document will be a document of the *Scottish* Reformation. In responsibility towards what was 325 years later offered " to the whole population of Scotland," I am letting John Knox and his friend speak in their *Confessio Scotica* of 1560. This is not to take the form of an historical analysis of the Scottish Confession, but that of a theological paraphrase and elucidation of the document as it speaks to-day and as we to-day by a careful objective examination of its content can hear it speak. I say " to-day " advisedly. I am aware that in present-day Scotland the *Confessio Scotica* has no longer any significance as a standard of the church. Naturally it has no significance in that sense for me either. On that account we shall be in a position to listen to what it has to say all the more impartially. The Confession of a church, if it was once a good confession, cannot lose its message just because it has lost its significance as a standard of the church. He that has ears to hear, hears it even then. And the confession of John Knox is a good confession—and, moreover, in many respects a very original and interesting confession. And besides, even if it had significance as a standard of the church, it could not even then be understood as a code of doctrine binding us by its letters and sentences. Reformation teaching knows of no law set over it except the spiritual law of the Scripture, which must be heeded ever anew. Reformation teaching neither can nor will insinuate itself between us and Scripture. The *Confessio Scotica* itself declares in Article 18 : " The interpretation [of Scripture] we confesse, neither appertaines to private nor publick persone, nether zit to ony Kirk for ony preheminence or prerogative personallie or locallie, quhilk ane hes above ane uther, bot apperteines to the Spirite of God, be the quhilk also the Scripture was written." And it applies this to itself in the words of the preface, " Protestand that gif onie man will note in this our confessioun onie artickle or sentence repugnand to Gods Halie word, that it wald pleis him of his gentleness and for christian charities sake to admonish us of the same in writing ; and we upon our honoures and fidelitie, be Gods grace do promise unto him satisfactioun fra the mouth of God, that is fra his haly scriptures, or else reformation of that quhilk he sal prove to be amisse." That means manifestly that when we associate ourselves with this document, we must at the same time remain free in relation to it—free to give heed to the Scripture itself. The *Confessio Scotica* wishes to be read and understood as a signpost pointing to Scripture. To understand it in any other sense would be to fail to understand it in its true and historical significance. Therefore the theological paraphrase and elucidation of the *Confessio Scotica*, that I would like to offer here, is to be a repetition, exposition and presentation of its text in the way in which according to its own purport it desires to be read and understood to-day—as a witness to Scripture and therefore in the light of Scripture, which authenticates but also criticises it. It goes without saying that my treatment of the text of the Confession is subjected to the same standard and ultimately to this standard *only*.

THE ONE GOD

(Art. 1*a*)

OF GOD

We confesse and acknawledge ane onelie God, to whom only we
must cleave, whom onelie we must serve, whom onelie we must
worship, and in whom onelie we must put our trust.

I

" We confesse and acknawledge *God* . . . ." So
begins the Scottish Confession. Who or what lies
hidden behind this word " God "—a word with which
indeed we are only too familiar ?   All confessions of
all churches and religions purport to treat of " God."
What is conceived by all other " believers," past,
present and future, whatever the manner, place and
date of their belief, is certainly not what the Scottish
Confession means by the object of its profession.
The Confession does not *conceive* its object at all, it
acknowledges it : " We confesse and acknawledge."
And before we have time to ask it how and where it
acknowledges God, it has already singled out a part of
this knowledge of God,—or should we not rather say
the whole of it ?—and placed it before us in the words
" We confesse and acknawledge *ane onelie* God." It
thus puts to us, so to speak, the counter question
whether we ourselves do not acknowledge this same
one and only God, and whether we have not 'long
known how and where He, the one and only God,

was to be acknowledged. But a Confession cannot wait for the assent of its hearers. *This*, it says, *this* is God, the one and only God, " to whom only we must cleave, whom onelie we must serve, whom onelie we must worship, and in whom onelie we must put our trust." The note struck here is characteristic of all confessions of the Reformed church ; the French and Dutch confessions for instance begin in an exactly similar way. Yet this note is struck with special emphasis in the Scottish Confession, and we shall meet it time and again in our text.

It will repay us to halt here for a moment and to consider this phrase " ane onelie God " carefully. It is not an innovation or a discovery of the sixteenth century which is put forward here, but it is certainly a renewal, a rediscovery and a restoration of knowledge long forgotten and denied. The voice of the Old Testament becomes articulate here once more, " Hear, O Israel, Jahweh our God is Jahweh the one and only God " (Deut. 6, 4). The voice of the New Testament becomes audible too, " We know that there is none other God but one " (1 Cor. 8, 4). So, too, the voice of the early church : " Deus si non unus est, non est " (Tert. *adv. Marc.* 1, 3). Therefore to speak of God is to speak of the one and-only God. To know God means to know the one and only God. To serve God means to serve the *one and only* God. This is what Reformed teaching brings to light again. In and along with everything else which it says, it says this also.

In saying this what does Reformed teaching mean ? It does not mean that God alone exists. It does not deny the world. It denies neither its variety nor its unity in itself, neither its splendour nor its fearful secrets, neither the profundity of nature nor the profundity of spirit. The world *exists*, but the world does not exist alone. And if the world does not exist alone, because it exists through God and therefore as having God behind, above and before it, as Him without whom it would not exist, so God does not exist alone, because the world exists through Him. It exists through Him, Who, without the world, would yet be in Himself no less what He is. The difference in the relation between them is this—God exists along with the world as its free creator, whereas the world exists along with God as the creation founded on His freedom. By recognising this difference we recognise God as the one and only God. At the conclusion of our confession we find the invocation, " Arise, O Lord, and let thy enimies be confounded . . ." Knowledge of the one and only God becomes possible and real, because this does happen, because God does " arise " and makes Himself visible in the world and distinguishes Himself *from* the world as its creator, thereby making the world visible and distinguishing it as His creation. Whatever the world may be as a whole and whatever separate entity may exist within the world—be it its final grounds and principles—this is not creative in the way in which God is creative, nor free as God is free, nor Lord as He is Lord. For it exists through God and, unlike God, does not possess its specific existence in itself. " We acknawledge ane onelie God "—that is the description of how we know the One Who becomes knowable in this distinction, consummated by Him Himself. Our knowledge will only be able to follow the drawing of this distinction. " Arise, O Lord." Our thought in so far as it follows this " arising " attains to this knowledge of God, and 'can attain to this knowledge alone. " We acknawledge ane onelie God "—this is no mere part of the knowledge of God, but rightly understood is itself the sum of all true knowledge of God and for that reason this sentence may legitimately stand at the head of the confession.

II

Let us, in the first place, make clear to ourselves the far-reaching importance of this sentence. I repeat, it does not mean the negation, the denial or the depreciation of that which is not God. But it does mean that this latter factor is criticised, *limited* and made *relative*. It says precisely that this factor is not God. Whatever else it may be, only illegitimately can it conduct itself as God, and only illegitimately can it be regarded and treated as God. Whatever else it may be, we are free to abandon it ; we are not compelled to serve it or worship it and we cannot in any sense or on any account put our hope of salvation in it. The greatness, beauty and importance which it may have in itself and also for us within the world is indisputable. That is expressly acknowledged in the New Testament passage previously cited, " There are (in heaven and on earth) gods many and lords many " (1 Cor. 8, 5). But these are gods so-called (λεγόμενοι θεοί) and the knowledge of the one and only God means that they are unmasked as such.

16

The god " so-called," which the proposition about the " ane onelie God " was designed to combat, is above all *man himself*. We cannot help seeing this to-day even more clearly than was possible in the sixteenth century before the Cartesian revolution had taken place. It is man's self-assertion which is the source of the possible or actual denial of the one and only God—not perhaps in the form that man denies the existence of the one and only God but very simply in the form that he identifies himself with the one and only God. Man can regard himself and treat himself as the measure of all things, just as if he were Creator or free or Lord like Him to whom he owes his being. He can therefore think that he dare not abandon himself but must serve and worship himself, and that he can therefore put his hope of salvation in himself. Without denying God, man can consider himself as having power over God. And not only can man do that, but he actually does it. Eritis sicut Deus. This voice was heard and obeyed by man long before the time of Descartes. Now the knowledge of the one and only God means the *limiting* of this human self-assertion. " We acknawledge ane onelie God " means simply, we men are not gods or are merely gods so-called or make-believe gods. We are forced to retire within the bounds of our own creatureliness and our own human nature. The modern world has failed to hear the warning of the Reformed confession precisely at this point and has thought fit to exchange the mediæval conception of the world as geocentric for the much more naïve conception of the world as anthropocentric.

The gods so-called, which the proposition about the " ane onelie God " was designed to combat, are, however, also the gods and godheads of all the human ideologies and mythologies, philosophies and religions. With the well-known ambition of a devoted father, man decks the children of his self-assertion with the same authority with which he has previously decked himself. These are the systems by means of which he proposes—at least in phantasy and fancy—to exercise his divine freedom and lordship. They might also be described as costumes, each one more beautiful than the other, which man dons in turn in his rôle as the one and only reality. And just as fathers must sometimes accommodate themselves to their children, and just as each costume constrains the actor to adopt a definite attitude, so the systems woven in man's phantasy and fancy come to possess and keep a definite power over him. His conception of the world and thus his world become full of ideas and principles, points of view scientific, ethical and æsthetic, axioms, self-evident truths social and political, certainties conservative and revolutionary. They exercise so real a dominion and they bear so definitely the character of gods and godheads, that not infrequently devotion to them actually crystallises into mythologies and religions. (Universities are the temples of these religions.) But each one of these claims at the moment to be the one and only reality with monopoly over all systems. It is now considered impossible to abandon them either. Service and honour are offered them also and it is believed that the hope of salvation should be put in them. To recognise the one and only God means to make all these systems relative. "We acknawledge ane onelie God" means that the principles and objects of these systems, whatever they may be, are in reality no gods or at best gods so-called. Are they to be annihilated? Perhaps not at all, perhaps not yet. But the end of their authority is within sight. When the knowledge of God becomes manifest, they can no longer possess ultimate credibility, and real, serious and solemn reverence cannot be shown them any longer. "What askest thou Me concerning the good? One is good" (Matt. 19, 17). "The destruction of the gods" comes down upon them then. In any case they can henceforward prolong their existence only as symbols and hypotheses, perhaps as angels or as demons, perhaps only as ghosts and comical figures. This makes clear to us how it was possible for the early Christians to have been accused of atheism, and the Christian church would be in a better position if she had remained suspect of atheism in this sense of the word in modern times as well. All that we can say is that this is not the case. The church has much rather played a most lively part in the game of dressing up in different costumes a mere counterfeit of the one and only reality.

III

Knowledge of the truly one and only God gains this meaning when it is brought about by this truly one and only God Himself. God is the one and only One and proves Himself to be such by His being both the Author of His own Being and the source of all knowledge of Himself. In both these respects He differs from everything in the world. A God who could be known otherwise than through Himself, i.e. otherwise than through His revelation of Himself, would have already betrayed, eo ipso, that He was not the one and only one and so was not God. He would have betrayed Himself to be one of those principles underlying human systems and finally identical with man himself. But the *Confessio* speaks not of one of those principles nor of man but of God, and therefore of One through whom all things exist, and who wills to be known through no one except through Himself.

There exists a conception of the *unity* of all being in its totality. All human thought takes this into account. And this conception can even gain remarkable depth and richness by means of the conception of the *uniqueness* (the one-and-onlyness) of all being in its individuality. All human thought has taken this also into account from the start. We may adopt this hypothesis of the one, and we may recognise and formulate this cosmic problem of the one as such. Yet in doing so we have done absolutely nothing that would have even a distant connection with the knowledge of God. The secret fire of all or almost all philosophies and religions is kindled by the charm of the idea of mathematical unity, intensified by the charm of the principle of individuality—not to speak of the fire which political domination has needed, whenever the world or a part of it has been ripe for such a domination. But a wrong is done and a strange fire is brought to the altar, if men seek to kindle the fire of the knowledge of God by this charm—and from time to time the Fathers did do this. Thomas

Aquinas's sentence that " Deus non est in aliquo genere " (*Sum. Theol.* 1, Ques. 3, Art. 5) must be rigorously applied to the genus " unity " or " uniqueness " (one-and-onlyness) also. What falls under this genus is as such not God, even if it were the ultimate and highest conceivable or perceptible unity of the world. The God of Mohammed is an idol like all other idols, and it is an optical illusion to characterise Christianity along with Islam as a " monotheistic " religion.

True knowledge of the one and only God, knowledge of Him in the sense of our Confession, is based on the fact that the one and only God makes Himself known. Everything is through Him Himself or is not at all. He makes Himself known through Himself by distinguishing Himself *in* the world *from* the world. Otherwise He cannot be known at all. He can be known, because He arises—" Arise, O Lord "—in human form and therefore in a way that is visible and audible for us, i.e. as the eternal Son of God in the flesh, the one and only God in Whom we have been called to believe, Jesus Christ. He proves Himself in Jesus Christ to be the One to whom no one and nothing is to be preferred or even to be compared, " cuius neque magnitudini neque maiestati neque virtuti quidquam, non dixerim praeferri, sed nec comparari potest " (Novatian, *De Trin.* 31). Because He manifests Himself thus, He makes Himself knowable to us not through revelation of some sort or other, but through the fact of His self-revelation. On this Paul also has based the knowledge of God as the one and only God in contrast to the many " gods " further on in the passage already quoted. " But to us there is but one God the Father, of whom are all things, and we in Him ; and one Lord Jesus Christ by whom are all things, and we by Him." This " *but* " which belongs to the self-revelation of the one and only God, is what brings about " the destruction of the gods," of which we have spoken.

IV

Let us conclude by putting this to the test. And in this connection it is quite legitimate to turn our thoughts to the story of Elijah and the prophets of Baal on Mount Carmel (1 Kings 18). Which will prove itself to be the one and only reality—man and his principles or He whom the Confession contrasts to them on the ground of His self-revelation ? Is *man* able to sustain his part as the one and only reality and thus do justice to his claim to freedom and lordship ? This he is unable to do, because in the very playing of this part he has to furnish and fill his picture of the world with the objective principles above mentioned, and they in their turn win and exercise dominion over him ; for he has to live in the world which corresponds to his picture of it. They will remind him forcibly enough of the fact that he is not the one and only reality and that he is not free and does not possess any power. Man must live as a slave to those powers whom he has made his masters. But do these world powers then—nature or spirit, destiny or reason, desire or duty—possess the character of being the one and only reality and therefore that of lordship ? And which of them really does so ? All previous experience seems to teach that their mutual conflict does not reach any decision. But even if a decision were one day to be reached, which of these world powers could—or could they all together ?—be powerful enough to make a real prisoner of man and of human self-assertion ? Spirit, nature, reason, duty, desire—which of these has power to make man completely prisoner ? And though man is powerless to maintain himself as the one and only reality, does he not at least possess sufficient power to set his own subjective self-assertion against the world powers which are after all the offspring of his mind ? Does he not therefore possess sufficient power at least to call in question their claim to be the one and only reality ? When and where did mankind really entrust or commit themselves totally and without reservation to nature or spirit, destiny or reason, desire or duty ? Man may not know how to escape them, but he does know how to make reservations for himself in relation to them, " si fractus illabitur orbis, impavidum ferient ruinae." The conflict between these two parties, man and the powers of his world, over their right to be the one and only reality cannot be settled but ends in indecision. But the conflict is settled already where the parties to the conflict are man on the one hand and the one and only God in His self-revelation on the other. As these two stand face to face, there is decision, a command and a choice which commit man at this point, where man stands before God in His revelation. A claim to lordship is put forward possessing the power to achieve its end. Here man can obey completely, trust completely and commit himself completely and here he can worship. Here man will be able to recognise the one and only God by the fact that He is the one and only God, and here He is the one and only God because He reveals Himself as such. To achieve this result as the conclusion of this test is something which is in no one's power. The decision, with which it does reach its conclusion, is faith in Jesus Christ, and in saying that we are saying once more that the one and only God Himself is He Who reveals Himself as the one and only God. But in saying that we are saying also what is decisive—what in the sense of the Confession must be said about the words " We acknawledge ane onelie God."

THE MAJESTIC, THE PERSONAL GOD

(Art. 1*b*)

Who is Eternall, Infinit, Unmeasurable, Incomprehensible, Omnipotent, Invisible : ane in substance, and zit distinct in thre
personnis, the Father, the Sone, and the holie Gost.

I

Reformed teaching gives a twofold answer to the
question, " Who is the one God ? " In the first
place, He is *majesty* (He is eternal, infinite, immeasure-
able, incomprehensible, omnipotent, invisible, as the
Confession says). Secondly, He is a *Person* (since in
His simple, majestic essence He is the Father, the Son
and the Holy Spirit).

It is well to note at the start that this explanation
is introduced in the Latin translation of the Confession by the expression " *eundem* etiam *credimus*
. . . " The knowledge of the one and only God, the
knowledge *that* He is and *who* He is, is the knowledge
of *faith*. Faith knowledge in the sense used by
Reformed teaching does not mean a knowledge which
is based merely on feeling, which is peculiar to the
individual and which therefore has no binding character for others. On the contrary, no more objective
and strict form of knowledge can exist, and no type of
knowledge can lay claim more definitely to universal
validity than the knowledge of faith. It is certainly

true that it differs completely from anything else which man calls knowledge, not only in its content, but in its mode of origin and form as well. But this difference consists precisely in the fact that it is bound, a fact which excludes all arbitrariness and chance. The very question " Who is God ? " is not one of those questions which man puts to himself and is able either to put or not to put to himself. On the contrary, on every occasion that he raises it in earnest, he is *compelled* to raise it, because without his ever coming to think of it of his own accord, this question *is put* to him in such a way that it must be faced, and cannot be evaded. Also in answering it he will not be able to choose, but he will have to obey—to read off, spell out and decipher the answer which is laid down for him. Faith knowledge is knowledge through revelation. And that simply means that it is a type of knowledge which is unconditionally bound to its object. And it is only to this object—only to God—that human thought can be bound in this way, since God Himself has bound it to Himself. " Jesus said unto them, Come ye after me " (Mk. 1, 17). " And they forsook all and followed Him " (Luke 5, 11). The binding of obedience to command here is the basis of the knowledge of faith. " And they forsook all and followed Him " is the foundation of the knowledge of God. And when this knowledge *speaks*, the binding of obedience to command remains. It does not speak with the freedom from obligation characteristic of a monologue or of what we call a discussion. It speaks with responsibility towards Him from whom it has heard what it has to say, as it completes a *liturgical*

26

act. It is only subsequently, incidentally and really unintentionally that what is said in the knowledge of faith can also be said as something for which we are responsible to men and have to justify before them. But what is said in the knowledge of faith is rigorous, effective and universally valid for men, just because it is said originally and really to God and not to men.

II

Let us try now to estimate the *formal* character of faith knowledge, i.e. knowledge through revelation, the knowledge that God is Majesty and that He is a Person. Compared with the French, Dutch and other confessions the Scottish Confession shows originality by linking together directly the confession of faith in the God who is *hidden* in His eternity, infinity, etc., and the confession of faith in the same God as He is *known* to us as the God Who is Three in One, Father, Son and Holy Spirit. What does it mean by placing together the two—the God who is hidden and the God who is known ?

When, in the first place, we look from the second truth towards the first, the meaning is as follows. Precisely because God makes Himself known to us in an unsurpassably intimate and definite way as the Father, the Son and the Holy Spirit, He meets us as the One who is hidden, the One about Whom we must admit that we do not know what we are saying when we try to say who He is. Who is the Father, Whose children we are called to be in Jesus Christ ? Who is He whom the Father has delivered up for us as His only Son, that in Him and through Him amends might be made for all the evil we do ? Who is the Holy Spirit, the Spirit of this Father and this Son, qui procedit ex patre filioque, through Whom we participate in all these benefits ? We must answer that this One Being is eternal, infinite, immeasurable, incomprehensible, omnipotent and invisible. By each and all of these words we mean that He is *above* us, *above* space and time, and *above* all concepts and opinions and all potentialities. When we use all these words, we are praising His freedom and power. But what kind of freedom is that which is not bound to space and time or any potentiality known to man ? By using all these words, we call Him the Lord, Jahweh Kyrios, but to what Lord will we compare Him ? And how are we then to comprehend Him, when we call Him Lord ? Thus God's revelation is precisely His revelation as the *hidden* God. And therefore faith in God's revelation can only give a very *humble* answer to the question " Who is God ? " and it is faith which will confess God as the God of majesty and therefore as the God unknown to us. It is faith in God's revelation which is deadly fear of God's mystery, because it sees how God Himself veils Himself in mystery. Scepticism, which thinks that it also knows that God is hidden, has not reached the point of being such fear unto death. Scepticism has not been taught by God Himself that He is hidden, but is a human answer to a human question. One must know the darkness of Sinai and of Calvary and must have faith, to know the God who is *above* us and His hidden nature.

And now let us look from the first truth towards the second. This unknown God above us Who is known to faith, is not an unknown natural law, or an unknown cosmic riddle or unknown fate. He *deals* with man in the very act of confronting him in the darkness of Sinai and Calvary. By being above him, He is *with* him. By being far from him, He is also *near* him. Our words falter when we praise God's freedom and might, because they are greater than all that we can understand by freedom and might. But it is right and necessary so to praise Him, since it is in His majesty that He has given Himself to be *known*, has *spoken* of Himself and *attested* Himself as Him *by* whom, *through* whom and *for* whom we exist. (We exist *by* Him—for we are created by Him. We exist *through* Him—for we are sustained and supported through the peace which He grants us. We exist *for* Him—for we are destined for a future which lies beyond, for a beyond which lies in the future, and which consists in perfect life with Him.) In His whole incomprehensible majesty He is no stranger to us, but the Lord who in fullest reality surrounds us on all sides.

And though our words falter when we call Him Lord, yet He Himself has given us the ground and occasion for uttering these faltering words and He has given us the ground and occasion for being perfectly certain of His Lordship in the midst of the uncertainty which is and remains our portion. Moreover, we are aware of His being hidden and therefore of the faltering nature of our words and thus of our uncertainty only by His having made Himself known to us as the one who dwells in majesty, the Father, the Son and the Holy Spirit. Thus faith in God's revelation can in all lowliness of spirit give nothing but a very *courageous* answer to the question " Who is God ? " without thereby ceasing to be fear unto death before the hiddenness of God. It is faith which will confess God as the One Who possesses a name and therefore is a person and therefore is the God with Whom we are very well acquainted. It is faith which holds its ground before God, and in all soberness takes the presence of God into account, consorts with Him, listens and speaks to Him. It is faith which knows God as a child knows its father, or as a brother his brother or even as a man knows himself. There does exist also a speculative optimism which thinks it is very well acquainted with God in nature, in history and in the heart of man. But this optimism has, in principle, not reached the simplicity in which man may have intercourse with God as the God Whom he knows. It has not yet been taught by God Himself that we may really have intercourse with Him, because He has come so near to us. Such optimism is only a human answer to a human question. Something else must be known before we can say God is near us. To believe in the God who is near us and to recognise God's presence, we must be brought with Israel out of Egypt and must know the grace of Good Friday, Easter and Pentecost, and must have faith.

III

It is necessary to make clear what is contained in the conception " *Person* " if we intend to speak of

God's personality. The doctrine of the Trinity, assumed in the *Confessio Scotica* as an indisputable truth, does not mean that in God there are three subjects. What it does say is that from eternity and to eternity God is *the* Subject, *the* Person, who establishes Himself and is founded on Himself, the Son on the Father, the Spirit on the Father and the Son. He is thrice named, and thrice truly exists as the *One* God, the *one* Subject, the *one* Person, but *the* Person who begets Himself, proceeds from Himself and Himself is master of His own existence and essence. As this Subject who is three in one, in virtue of the incomparable freedom and power in which He is what He is, without standing in need of any other being or predicate—as *this* Person God can and must be free and therefore have dominion over all existence which differs from His existence and over all essence which differs from His essence. Precisely as *this* Person He is *Lord*, is *above* us, the God of majesty, the hidden God.

God is therefore a Person in a way quite different from that in which we are persons. Our relations to others condition what we are. Our existence as persons requires a world around us with the conditions and limitations which such a world imposes. We are not persons possessed of majesty, and therefore we ought not to think that we are, though sometimes we do. Thus God is personal, but personal in an *incomprehensible* way, in so far as the conception of His personality surpasses all our views of personality. This is so, just because He and He alone is a true, real and genuine person. Were we to overlook this and

31

try to conceive God in our own strength according to our conception of personality, we would make an idol out of God. We will avoid this, if in dealing with the question " Who is God ? " we keep to the answer given by God Himself and therefore to God's revelation and thus to the knowledge of faith.

IV

But it is also necessary to make clear what is contained in the conception " *Majesty*," if it is to be applied to God. It is easy to misunderstand the Confession, as if by enumerating a number of attributes such as the eternal, infinite, etc., which are assumed to be perfectly clear, it seeks to offer a universally intelligible philosophy of the Absolute, to which the doctrine of the Trinity is in some amazing way to be attached. On this view the name Father, Son and Holy Spirit is just a special predicate of a subject with which we are already familiar, namely the Absolute. The traditional practice, which goes far back in theology, of speaking *first* of God's essence and attributes and only *then* of the three-in-oneness, has helped to bring about this misunderstanding. But God's majesty is to be measured just as little by the standard of the human idea of the Absolute as God's personality is to be measured by the standard of our view of human personality. The human idea of the Absolute, which we are accustomed to think of as identical with God, is the reflection of the world, and in the end the disastrous reflection of human personality. Once again, if we had equated this idea with God, we

32

would have set up the image of an idol. We have not to draw our knowledge of who God is from what we think we know about eternity, infinity, omnipotence and invisibility as conceptions which bound our thought. On the contrary, we have to draw our knowledge of eternity, infinity, omnipotence and invisibility from what we can know about God, from what God has said to us about Himself. If we choose to take the first way or the various ways into which this first way is generally divided—the famous via negationis, the via eminentiae, and via causalitatis—we could as easily conclude with the definition " God is nothing " as with the second one " God is everything " or the third " God is the One in everything." And with it all, what we have defined, would not be God. On the contrary, we would have defined in one way or another the essence of that which is not God, we would have defined the creature, and in the end, as Ludwig Feuerbach has irrefutably shown, the essence of man himself. If we do not wish to end by really defining ourselves, when we think that we are defining God, we can only take the second way and therefore hold fast to the *incomprehensible* majesty in which God meets us in His revelation, the majesty of His person as Father, Son and Holy Spirit. *His* majesty consists in His being the archetypal Person, i.e. truly, really and genuinely a person. As a *divine* Person, He has freedom over Himself and over all things, as we saw above. But as a *Person*, in distinction from those images of our imagination, He is One Who knows and wills, Who acts and speaks, Who as an " I " calls me " Thou " and Whom I can call

C   33

" Thou " in return. This is the true name of God declared by Him Himself, and in it we must seek also the whole mystery of His majesty. Apart from this name it would have to remain completely hidden from us.

THE GLORY OF GOD AND THE GLORY OF MAN

(Art. 1c-2b)

Be whom we confesse and beleve all thingis in hevin and eirth, aswel Visible as Invisible, to have been created, to be reteined in their being, and to be ruled and guyded be his inscrutable Providence, to sik end, as his Eternall Wisdome, Gudnes, and Justice hes appoynted them, to the manifestatioun of his awin glorie.

ART. II

OF THE CREATIOUN OF MAN

We confesse and acknawledge this our God to have created man, to wit, our first father *Adam*, to his awin image and similitude, to whome he gave wisdome, lordship, justice, free-wil, and cleir knawledge of himselfe, sa that in the haill nature of man there culd be noted no imperfectioun.

I

The Reformed church and Reformed theology have never spoken about God and man as if God were everything and man were nothing. That is a caricature of Reformed teaching and we have already rejected such a preposterous view in passing, in our second lecture. By slightly altering a sentence formulated there we can say now " God alone is God but God is not alone." God alone possesses divine glory, but alongside His glory there exists a glory which belongs to the world and to man. The world and man exist—in the way in which their existence is

35

possible alongside God—but they do exist. They exist in the truth and independence, in the distinctiveness and beauty and with the teleological character, which it is *possible* for them to possess alongside God. But they do in point of fact exist in this glory which they possess alongside God. They exist in this their peculiar glory under the definite *ordinance*, by which they do not possess their glory *from* themselves, but receive it from God, and do not possess it *for* themselves, but in order that the glory of God might be the greater thereby; but under this ordinance they themselves do possess a peculiar glory, which it is quite certain God does not grudge them, rob them of or even diminish. Only by the *overthrowing* of this ordinance can they lose their peculiar glory. If they wish to possess it from themselves and for themselves, they will certainly cease to possess it. They have then fallen victim to shame, folly and death. On the other hand, if this ordinance is *restored*, in and with it the glory of the world and of man is restored also. It holds good therefore that in its overthrow and in its restoration also, the glory of the world and of man is founded on the glory of God, fully determined by it and bound by it.

II

Let us proceed from the simple fact that in the revelation of God in Jesus Christ, God and man meet, and therefore are really together. We shall see later that we have to use an even stronger expression than this, and speak of God being one with man. But at this point the more guarded conception of God and man being together is sufficient. The name of Israel's expected Messiah is, according to Isaiah 7, 14, Immanuel, i.e. God with us. This teaches us as our first point that *God is not alone.* God's revelation presupposes that there exists distinct from God a world *in which* He can reveal Himself and *someone to whom* He can reveal Himself. In His own eternal Being there is no need for any revelation and there can be no revelation there, because there is nothing hidden, since God is eternally manifest to Himself. If there is a revelation of God, then there exists alongside God an " other " which is not God. Revelation as the fact that God and man are really together is itself the evidence of the reality of the divine *creation.* By this it is revealed—apart from everything which revelation may mean in itself—that the world is not nothing and not mere appearance. In this fact, man above all, as the one to whom God turns in His revelation, is affirmed and taken seriously in his existence, is addressed as God's vis-à-vis and partner and thereby honoured in his independence and acknowledged in the distinctiveness and teleological character of his created being. We cannot believe God's revelation without at the same time being given to see the outlines of the reality of the world and of our own reality, which, though mysterious, ambiguous and puzzling, are yet unmistakable. This reality is not one which is founded or rests on itself, but is *created* by God But for that very reason it is a reality *saved* from nothingness and *distinguished* from appearance. More than the glory of the *creature* cannot be ascribed to it in the light of revelation. But *this* glory cannot

37

be denied it in the light of revelation. God in His majesty as the Father, Son and Holy Spirit requires no other being and possesses all majesty in Himself, yet He does not content Himself with Himself and thus with the glory which He possesses perfectly in Himself. On the contrary, His glory overflows in His creating, sustaining and governing the world and in the world man, and in His giving to this His creation the glory of being the reflection (imago) of His own glory. The love of God consists in this, that though He does not need the world and man He will not be without them. He will not be without this reflection (imago) of His glory, or without the glory which creation is appointed to give back to Him again. And the peculiar glory of the creation is to possess this appointed destiny and to be obedient to it by virtue of God's free love.

III

Let us return again to the fact of the meeting of God and man in God's revelation in Jesus Christ. This being together of God and man is grace. It is something which man needs. But it is God who has sought man, that they might be thus together and not man who has sought God. This teaches us as our second point that *the creation is under a debt of gratitude to God*. God's revelation presupposes that the world and man stand in need of their Creator, that they have no power over Him and that He creates, sustains and governs them with divine freedom. They do not possess their glory in themselves but in their being permitted to reflect this divine glory by

virtue of the overflowing glory of God. They possess
it therefore in showing themselves grateful to God.
At this point we must make certain delimitations.
Following the example of the Nicæan symbol the
Confessio Scotica terms the object of creation " all
thingis in hevin and eirth, aswel *Visible as Invisible*."
This expresses the clear, correct and important fact
that the world of *spirit* is no less created by God
than the world of *nature* and the world of nature no
less than the world of spirit. There would be no
point in preferring one of these realms to the other, as
if spirit (or according to others, nature) had its glory
in itself, and therefore did not stand in need of the
grace of the Creator. Neither of these realms stands
in direct relation to God, however highly idealistic
philosophy may prize spirit or the opposing material-
istic philosophy may prize nature. And neither of
these realms is absolved from the duty of gratitude,
however much the idealists may despise nature and
the materialists spirit. But this is true also mutatis
mutandis of the antithesis between *coming into being*
and *passing away*. Both of these extol the glory of
God—not only the majesty of what we call growth,
progress and fulfilment of life, but also the darkness
of what we call decay, destruction and death. On
the other hand, it would be the sign of a narrow out-
look to look for God's glory only on the dark side of
creation and not on the bright side also. Both coming
into being and passing away stand in equal need of
the overflowing grace of the Creator, in order to possess
their own particular glory. The same is true also of
a third antithesis—the antithesis between the law of

necessity which we see governs all created life, and the *freedom* which we are summoned continually to manifest in the midst of this necessity. The summons of freedom is one whose universal claim we can as little gainsay as we can that of necessity. But the need for grace from the Creator is not greater in the one and less in the other. Freedom has no less glory of its own than necessity and necessity shares in the overflowing glory of the Creator in no lesser sense than freedom. The distinctions which we draw by means of such conceptions within the world created by God can be justified and helpful. But they are, at all events, provisional and relative. The ordinance of which we spoke is valid for all levels of the world— for all the heights as well as for all the depths. It is the ordinance of gratitude—" We believe *all* thingis in hevin and eirth, . . . to have been created, to be reteined in their being, and to be ruled and guyded be his inscrutable Providence, to sik end, as his Eternall Wisdome, Gudnes, and Justice hes appoynted them, to the manifestatioun of his awin glorie."

IV

Let us return once more to God's revelation in Jesus Christ. It is man who meets God here and it is man whom God is with here. Why does God not meet with Sirius or the rock crystal ? Or with the violet by the roadside or with the boa-constrictor ? Yes, why not ? But this is not what we are asked. The revelation of God in Jesus Christ—in the man Jesus Christ—is what alone distinguishes man, yet definitely distinguishes him within the rest of creation. We will not be guilty of the presumption of asserting that it is man who is specially appointed and qualified to receive the divine revelation. From what source could we know that ? But we can and must establish that it is man for whom the divine revelation is appointed. This teaches us a third point, that *Man has been called to present to the Creator the gratitude of the creation.*

The special position of man will best be defined in this guarded way. We cannot ascribe to ourselves more than what is the significance and purpose of the whole creation. We exist for " the manifestatioun of God's awin glorie." We possess our glory in serving the glory of God. We cannot know whether there may not be other beings who—perhaps in a far more perfect way than man—present to the Creator the gratitude due to Him from His creation. We are certainly not always wrong, if we believe we hear a song of praise to God in the existence also of Sirius and the rock crystal, of the violet and the boa-constrictor. But however that may be, we can know with regard to ourselves that we are not excused if we are not grateful—for in our existence as men we are certainly called to such gratitude. In the creation story in the Bible (Gen. 1, 26 ff.)—a passage adopted by the *Confessio Scotica*—we read " God created man ad imaginem et similitudinem ipsius," i.e. to be the image and likeness of Himself. This is misunderstood already in the Greek translation of the Old Testament — the Septuagint—and it is to be feared that the *Confessio Scotica* also fell into this misunderstanding,—as if what was described here was a condition or quality of being God's exact likeness, imparted to man at his creation and attaching to his existence thenceforward, so that we would have to ask in what respect this condition of being like God is really to be perceived now in man as man, or in what respect it was to be perceived in Adam. We would then have to ask if for example man's reason or his humanity was the image of God. For answers of this nature men will seek in vain. For the text speaks not of a quality, but of that for which man's " nature " is *appointed* in his existence, life and action. Man is appointed to be, and it is his glory to be, the image of God, to reflect His glory and therefore to be grateful to Him. It is as *man* that he is appointed for this. And therefore he is appointed to *recognise* God's glory and so to *act* as to give God the glory, since in these consist human existence, life and action. He is appointed to recognise that God is the one and only Lord and to act in a way which takes this into account. He is to recognise God's majestic Person and to act as one responsible to this majestic Person. We cannot know if this recognition and this action, for which man is appointed, is more pleasing to God than the roaring of the sea, or the gentle falling of snow flakes. Once again we are not asked this. But what we can know is that at any rate we are summoned so to know and act, summoned to the knowledge of God and the service of God as certainly as we men quâ men are called to be His image and to show Him gratitude— the same gratitude which the whole creation owes Him. The sea and the snowflakes owe Him this gratitude too, but *our* gratitude can take only the form of the knowledge of God and the service of God ; for we are not snowflakes or drops of water. And in this form *our* gratitude will be directed towards the Creator and Lord of the *whole* earth, the Creator of the sea and the boa-constrictor. How could we honour Him, if not as the One who has also created all other creatures for His glory ? This is the source of the confidence in which we may move about in the midst of the whole world, as we wander through its heights and depths. We cannot have confidence in 'any creature, since we can have confidence in God alone, but we can and should have confidence in the case of every creature in its Creator and Lord. But to do this, to be able to live a life of trust in God in this dark world, we must do what *we* are under an obligation to do—we must show gratitude for the unspeakable grace of *our* creation and must reflect God's glory, and this is effected by our recognising Him and doing what is right in His sight.

V

Let us note in conclusion that the whole subject would consist in abstract conjectures and reflections devoid of any significance for life and also destined to break down at once as empty speculations, if they sought to be anything else than an exposition of the fact that God has revealed Himself to man in Jesus Christ. What do we know from any other source about " God," the " world " and " Man," and their mutual relations ? We know absolutely nothing, and everything becomes confused myth and wild metaphysic as soon as we turn aside from the statement of that fact by which God Himself has confirmed, explained and laid down the relationship of God, the world and man, and God's ordinance. By God's taking thought for man in Jesus Christ, now as in the past, He has provided us with knowledge about the creating, sustaining and governing of the world and man and about His glory and ours. Any book other than the Gospel, which we might open here, in order to find out about God, the world and man, could only lead us astray. It was no mere chance that the *Confessio Scotica* in its exposition of the Creation of man and his special appointment to be God's image, did not use the word God abstractly but said concretely *Our* God, Immanuel. To learn to see the Creator and Lord of all in " Our God," Immanuel, Jesus Christ, is the problem of the Christian doctrine of creation, a problem which is difficult and yet easy, easy and yet difficult.

THE WAY OF MAN

(Art. 2c-3)

Fra quhilk honour and perfectioun, man and woman did bothe fal : the woman being deceived be the Serpent, and man obeying the voyce of the woman, both conspyring against the Soveraigne Majestie of GOD, who in expressed words had before threatned deith, gif they presumed to eit of the forbidden tre.

ART III

OF ORIGINAL SINNE

Be quhilk transgressioun, commonlie called Original sinne, wes the Image of GOD utterlie defaced in man, and he and his posteritie of nature become enimies to GOD, slaves to Sathan, and servandis unto sin. In samekle that deith everlasting hes had, and sall have power and dominioun over all that have not been, ar not, or sal not be regenerate from above : quhilk regeneratioun is wrocht be the power of the holie Gost, working in the hartes of the elect of GOD, ane assured faith in the promise of GOD, reveiled to us in his word, be quhilk faith we apprehend Christ Jesus, with the graces and benefites promised in him.

I

Articles 2 and 3 of our Confession contain an innovation of their own, which is at once important and instructive. According to the procedure customary in almost all ancient and modern dogmatics and followed by the other Reformed confessions of the sixteenth century, there is a special and independent doctrine of man's *sin*. But the *Confessio Scotica* has not adopted this procedure. What it has to say about Adam's fall it says in Article 2 in connection with the doctrine of the destiny appointed for man by " our God." And what it has to say about what is called original sin appears in Article 3 as an introductory clause to the doctrine of saving faith in Jesus Christ, brought about by the Holy Spirit, a doctrine which is here directly expressed for the first time. The Scottish Confession indicates in the strongest of terms the horror of the fact that man became and is a sinner, by setting it clearly in a connection in which it is both preceded and followed ' by the grace of God, the Creator and Reconciler of men. But it is in this *connection* that it occurs. The authors of our confession manifestly wished to avoid considering even for a moment this fact of sin separately and as such. That man is *against God* is true and important and has to be taken seriously. But what is even truer, more important and to be taken more seriously is the other fact that God in Jesus Christ is *for man*. And it is only from the standpoint of the latter fact that it can be seen how true and important the former is, and how seriously it must be taken. We have reason therefore for allowing ourselves to be guided by our text and for thinking the matter out from this point of view.

In our second and third lectures we became acquainted with the Reformed doctrine of God and in the fourth with the Reformed doctrine of God and man. If there were a special Reformed doctrine of *man*, a special Reformed anthropology, it could in point of fact only consist in the doctrine of *sin*. For man in his separation from God and in his distinctive character over against God is sinful man, i.e. man who is missing his way and violating the ordinance of his existence. This missing of his way consists in the fact that he is not content with his own human glory but grasps at God's glory, in order himself to be like God—as the Bible in Genesis 3 describes it. And what he achieves by taking this way and obeying the words " eritis sicut Deus " is the loss of his own glory also. But is not the *Confessio Scotica* right when it refuses to consider this particular occurrence in the abstract ? God would not be God if He left man to his own devices on this evil way of his, nor would He be God if man's attack on His glory were allowed to succeed and the overthrow of man's glory were allowed to become complete. If the history of man as such and by itself would go to prove that God is not God, the history of the man Jesus Christ proves that God is God. It proves that God does *not* will that human history should take its own course, and that, confronted with man's action and in spite of it, He does *not* allow this to happen. It is only too true that man goes his way, the way of Adam. But it is a great deal truer that God goes this way of man's *with* him, makes it *His* own way and thereby *changes* it, makes it an entirely *different* way. He makes the way of man's rebellion the way of His own victory, the way of destruction the way of salvation and the way of the overthrowing of His ordinance the way of its restoration. But if this is the case, then the truth of *man's* way can only be seen and understood if viewed from the greater truth of *God's* way with man. In

47

that case there cannot be a special Reformed doctrine of man, a special anthropology, which in the nature of the case could only be a doctrine of his sin. That being so, the history of man and his sin can only be presented in the way in which we see it presented in the history of the man Jesus Christ.

II

We read in Luke 5, 8 that Simon Peter, when face to face with a great miracle wrought by Jesus, fell on his knees before Him and said to Him, " Depart from me ; for I am a sinful man, O Lord." What distinguishes God's true revelation from all false and alleged revelation is that it is like a sudden flash of light in a dark room, and reveals that man, though created by God for His own glory and thus himself too possessed of glory, is in himself not light but darkness. Revelation is an act of God's compassion. So it reveals the plight of man as one who needs compassion. Revelation is an act of God's condescension. So it reveals the depth to which man has sunk. Who is the man Jesus Christ? Ecce homo—there He is in the position which all the prophets and apostles point to as the real incarnation of God, in which He reveals Himself. He is a child born in a stable and laid in a manger, " for they had no room in the inn," and in the end He is a malefactor hanged on the gallows. Thus there is one reason, and perhaps in the last resort only one reason, why the conception of a real revelation of God is alien and uncongenial to us and why we would be ready to hear of unreal revelations, but not of a true and real revelation of God. That reason is that this revelation, the revelation of God in Jesus Christ, necessarily means the discovery of the darkness which is man, of the plight in which he exists and the depths to which he has sunk, and this disclosure is what sharply contradicts his creation, the glory of God and his own glory. And what we are dealing with here is not simply the discovery of man's insignificance in face of the powers of nature and history, nor is it simply the discovery of the disparity between the finite and the infinite, nor is it simply the discovery of this or that mistake or error which man commits. All these are discoveries which man can make himself, and the history of religions shows that he has in fact done so long ago. And man is wont to accompany these discoveries with complaints of every kind, but these can cease as easily as they begin. But in the present case, man is not the subject but the object of the discovery. What is discovered here is not something which he *lacks* but who and what he *is*. Here he has nothing to complain about, but complaint is made against him. And here he is accused without regard for his age or his youth, his culture or his lack of culture, his morality or his lack of morality, his piety or his godlessness—it is Adam, man, who is accused here, Adam and Eve, man and woman—as the *Confessio Scotica* brings out very definitely. He and she are both in the position of " conspyring against the Soveraigne Majestie of God "—and in sixteenth-century Scotland, a place where there was no lack of conspiracy, men understood with exceptional clarity what that word

D   49

meant. They have both forsaken the ordinance in which they had their glory (alongside God's glory and for His glory). They have fallen away from the grace of creation in which they lived. They have rejected their vocation. They have refused God the gratitude which they owed Him. They have set themselves up as the lords of their life, as if they were Gods. Ecce homo—*such* is man as he is disclosed by God in His revelation. But the disclosure goes further. It now becomes clear what is the meaning and significance of his having *done* all this and of his having to *exist* as the person who has done all this. This brings us to what the old theology—and with it our Confession—calls Original Sin, the perversity in every man which follows from this perversion. For at what point can man's glory remain, when he is in rebellion against the glory of God? The very ordinance under which he as man was justified in his human nature, now becomes his judgement. " The Image of God [was] utterlie defaced in man." Man has now become a tarnished mirror in which the glory of God can no longer be reflected. To be man means *now* to be an enemy of God and this means to be the destroyer of one's own proper glory. To make use of the existence, dignity and freedom given us means *now* that we go farther along the well-trodden by-path, in our life as a whole and in all its details, and thus become ever more deeply and completely involved in our own corruption. To be in the world *now* means to be lost in the midst of powers, figures and events, which, after we became men without a lord, ceased likewise to have a lord, and so to have any

significance for us. To exist as God's creature means
now to be subject to death and eternal death at that,
to be subject to everlasting vanity which is the inevitable counterpart of the eternal efficaciousness of the
ordinance which we have broken. To repeat once
again, Ecce homo, *such* is man. And he is so beyond
recovery, i.e. it is impossible for him to annul even
one of these consequences of his sin. Above all it
is impossible for him to undo or to make amends for
his sin itself. Why can he not? The reason is that
it is his sin *against God*. That is why the accusation
brought against man in God's revelation does not
merely charge him with crimes or immoralities for
which he himself can and ought to make amends to
the best of his ability. It charges him with being
against God,—not merely of acting but of *being* against
God and of *being* so in all his actions. It is this that
he can neither undo nor make amends for. God's
revelation in Jesus Christ tells us this unambiguously
—for it consists in *God Himself* undoing and making
amends for our being against Him and for our sin.
If we believe this, it discloses to us the final horror
of sin and with it the impossibility of setting ourselves
free from it.

III

But this connection of sin and grace forbids us ever
to speak of sin as if it were the first or last word.
What would we know of the darkness, the plight and
the depths of human life without the light of revelation
which breaks through the darkness? How could
man know that he had sinned against God and that

he is against God, unless he knew that *God* is *for him ?*
How could man know that he himself can make amends
for absolutely nothing, unless he knew that *God
Himself* has made amends for the evil he does ? If
we know that we have sinned wantonly against God's
glory and have lost our own glory, then we already
know that God's glory, by proving true in the face of
our rebellion, has become only so much the *greater*,
and we know that He has *not* left man either to his
own devices on the road which leads to the destruction
of his own glory. If we know that we cannot save
ourselves, we know already that we are *saved* by God.
If we know that it is our sin and ourselves that were
condemned in the criminal's death suffered by the
man Jesus Christ on Calvary, then we know already
that our sin is *forgiven* us and that we ourselves are
set free from the sentence and judgement of God. If
we are afraid of the wrath of God and of our reproba-
tion, then we are already laying hold of the *promise* of
God and of our *election* and already believe in God's
compassion. If we confess and acknowledge, in the
words of the Calvinistic prayer, " that we have, alas,
gravely sinned from our youth up and to this present
hour by evil thoughts, words and deeds," then we
are already in God's arms and in His bosom. For
these words can only be uttered by a man who is
already there. Here we share not only in our glory
as men now restored to us, but far beyond this we
share also in that new glory which is founded on the
completely new order of grace as those who, through
God's coming in Jesus Christ, have been saved, won
and purchased to be called the *children* of God. For

it is only the children of God who can testify to their sin.

What is our sin? It is what we are and what we do, in spite of which God comes to us in the man Jesus Christ, as He came then to Peter in the ship. What is our debt? It is the showing of the gratitude which God has brought about and made efficacious for all of us in the man Jesus Christ. What is our punishment? It is the infinite agony which it cost God Himself to take our place in the man Jesus Christ, in order that we would not have to suffer. Is it nothing besides? No, nothing besides. In this way alone is there real, serious and Christian knowledge of our sin, debt and punishment—it is the essence of the *regeneration* of man as elected in God's free grace, which the Scottish Confession describes (at the end of Article 3) as man's only salvation, that it, since it is identical with *faith* in Jesus Christ awakened in us by the Holy Spirit, necessitates *this* knowledge of our sin, guilt and punishment and precludes any other.

IV

It remains for us expressly to set aside two misunderstandings. When we reflect on human life, no one can forbid us from forming a pessimistic—or maybe an optimistic—judgement about ourselves and mankind. We shall incline more to the former or to the latter according to our character and fortune. We shall now do the one and now the other according to the harmony or disharmony of our circumstances at the moment. But any sceptical or disparaging attitude towards human nature of which we feel convinced and consider legitimate, should not be confounded with the accusation, which according to Reformed teaching is levelled against man, and above all no attempt should be made to soften down this accusation by confounding it with such scepticism and disparagement. Christian doctrine cannot be disposed of by being called pessimism. Further, if a man permits himself to believe in the good in man and to believe that the human race is always going forward, he may do so. But he is not to confound such confidence in the progress of the human race with the promise of adoption to be God's children, which according to Reformed teaching is given to man. And even less is the promise to be confounded with such an amiable view. The Holy Spirit of God's Revelation in Jesus Christ does not wish to be confounded with any optimistic or pessimistic spirit of ours. The Holy Spirit brings His accusation against man even as viewed from the optimistic standpoint and we can thank God that His promise means to include man as viewed from the pessimistic standpoint. It is He alone, the Spirit of Jesus Christ the Son of God, who *brings about* the humiliation and exaltation of man, and it is He alone who *shows* us man in the humiliation and exaltation of which we have spoken. There can be only one relation between the Reformed teaching on sin, debt and punishment and the anthropology of the pessimists and optimists. They will be reminded by it not to forget that " man looketh on the outward appearance, but the Lord looketh on the heart."

54

THE REVELATION OF GOD IN JESUS CHRIST

(Art. 4-6)

ART IV

OF THE REVELATIOUN OF THE PROMISE

For this we constantlie beleeve, that GOD, after the feirfull and
horrible defectioun of man fra his obedience, did seek *Adam*
againe, call upon him, rebuke his sinne, convict him of the same,
and in the end made unto him ane most joyful promise, to
wit, *That the seed of the woman suld break down the serpents
head*, that is, he suld destroy the works of the Devill. Quhilk
promise, as it was repeated, and made mair cleare from time
to time ; so was it imbraced with joy, and maist constantlie
received of al the faithfull, from *Adam* to *Noe*, from *Noe* to
Abraham, from *Abraham* to *David*, and so furth to the incar-
natioun of *Christ Jesus*, all (we meane the faithfull Fathers
under the Law) did see the joyfull daie of *Christ Jesus*, and did
rejoyce.

ART V

OF THE CONTINUANCE, INCREASE, AND PRESERVATIOUN OF THE KIRK

We maist constantly beleeve, that God preserved, instructed,
multiplied, honoured, decored, and from death called to life,
his Kirk in all ages fra *Adam*, till the cumming of *Christ Jesus*
in the flesh. For *Abraham* he called from his Fathers cuntry,
him he instructed, his seede he multiplied ; the same he
marveilouslie preserved, and mair marveilouslie delivered
from the bondage and tyrannie of *Pharaoh* ; to them he gave
his lawes, constitutions and ceremonies ; them he possessed

55

in the land of *Canaan* ; to them after Judges, and after *Saul*, he gave *David* to be king, to whome hee made promise, that of the fruite of his loynes suld ane sit for ever upon his regall seat. To this same people from time to time he sent prophets, to reduce them to the right way of their God : from the quhilk oftentimes they declined be idolatry. And albeit that for their stubborne contempt of Justice, he was compelled to give them in the hands of their enimies, as befoir was threatned be the mouth of *Moses*, in sa meikle that the haly cittie was destroyed, the temple burnt with fire, and the haill land left desolate the space of lxx years : zit of mercy did he reduce them againe to *Jerusalem*, where the cittie and temple were reedified, and they against all temptations and assaultes of Sathan did abide, till the *Messias* come, according to the promise.

ART. VI

OF THE INCARNATION OF CHRIST JESUS

Quhen the fulnes of time came, God sent his Sonne, his eternall Wisdome, the substance of his awin glory in this warld, quha tuke the nature of man-head of the substance of woman, to wit, of a virgine, and that be operatioun of the holie Ghost : and so was borne the just seede of *David*, the Angell of the great counsell of God, the very *Messias* promised, whome we confesse and acknawledge *Emmanuel*, very God and very man, two perfit natures united, and joyned in one persoun. Be quhilk our Confessioun we condemne the damnable and pestilent heresies of *Arius, Marcion, Eutyches, Nestorius*, and sik uthers, as either did denie the eternitie of his God-head, or the veritie of his humaine nature, or confounded them, or zit devided them.

I

So far we have heard the Scottish Confession bear witness to the unity and the essence of God, to the ordinance which governs the relation between God,

56

the world and man and to the overthrow and restoration of that ordinance. What it has had to say on all these points, it has said on one definite presupposition and from one definite standpoint. The really decisive statements which we have met with would necessarily have remained completely unintelligible to us if we had not borne in mind and given the greatest possible emphasis to the fact that God and man must be spoken of in the way in which the Confession speaks of them " *because God reveals Himself to man in Jesus Christ.*" It is precisely this presupposition which distinguishes a Reformed confession from all confessions based on natural theology. This presupposition is explained in Art. 4-6. There we are told what is meant by this factor which dominates and determines everything, i.e. the revelation of God in Jesus Christ.

Let us try now to survey Articles 4-6. It is clear that the way in which the Confession speaks of this presupposition is to refer to *two histories*. It sees " the Revelation of God in Jesus Christ " in both these histories, considered by themselves and in their peculiar relation to one another. The *first* of these (dealt with in Articles 4 and 5) is the history of a definite section of the human race. It is thus the history of an extended period, embracing a whole range of ages and personages. In contrast to this, the second history (Art. 6) is confined to one single occurrence, happening, we might say, at one point in time ; its content consists of *one* period of time, *one* event and *one* person : " God sent his Sonne . . . in this warld." Yet these two histories in their complete and formal distinctiveness, and despite it, belong together; objectively considered they form a single history. For in both the same thing occurs—God proves His faithfulness in the midst of man's unfaithfulness. A way becomes manifest—the way of God's grace with sinful man. This way is seen and described in the *first* history as it presents itself when viewed from the side of man. Men are there, and there are many of them, a body or community continually being formed anew, a whole people. There happens now to them in the most varied way what happened to the first man Adam after his Fall : they are sought anew by God as the sinful men that they are, called by name, accused and condemned, but, moreover,—and here is the real content of the history of this remarkable people—they are consoled ever anew with the promise of a deliverer, and as the sinful men that they are, they are led, sustained, and supported by this consolation. They possess only the promise. They draw their life from a reality which transcends them. All they do is to stand and wait : they " did abide, till the *Messias* come." But what could they lack, since they possess the promise and are permitted to draw their life from this reality ? " All [the faithfull] . . . did see the joyfull daie of *Christ Jesus*, and did rejoyce " (John 8, 56). And this same way is seen and described in its true nature in the *second* history as the way which God goes with this people. The promise from which this people draws its life is no empty one, but is fulfilled. Therefore also the times of its history are fulfilled and are not empty. Its waiting and hoping are fulfilled and so too are the empty hands

58

which it holds out towards God. This people has a central point, a head,—this is what becomes manifest in the second history. The church whose life forms the content of that first history, has a Lord. In this Lord and Head, Jesus Christ, *God* and *man* (God and sinful man) are *one*. For this reason God maintains *fellowship* with all the men who belong to that people, whose Lord and Head is Jesus Christ.

Thus the revelation of God in Jesus Christ consists in the history of Israel seen as the history of God's Church together with the history of Jesus Christ seen as the history of God's becoming one with man. It was clearly from this position that the Scottish Confession spoke about the overthrow and the restoration of the glory of God and man, and about the original relation between them. The significance of everything which has been said in this connection is to be found in Israel and its Christ, just as Israel and its Christ are, as we shall see, at once the source and the subject of Reformed teaching.

II

In the view of the Scottish Confession the Old Testament with its presentation of the history of Israel is instruction given to the church about herself. God's revelation therefore tells us first—and this is the necessary and absolutely indispensable Old Testament side of the revelation—who and what we are ourselves—men whom God does not reject, but whom He cares for in His revelation.

That we are *judged* is a fact which precedes all

others, and runs like a scarlet thread through the whole history of Israel, beginning with that of Adam. Anti-Semitism is right. The Old Testament itself presents the matter in no other light. Israel is an evil people. Without a shadow of doubt they are sinners against God, His enemies and rebels against Him, whom He cares for in His revelation. But the church has neither time nor place for anti-Semitic modes of thought or speech. If she is the community of those who have fellowship with God, she recognises herself in her model, Israel. In the judgement passed by God on Israel she must therefore recognise the judgement passed upon herself. If she separated and withdrew herself from Israel and did not recognise herself as Israel, how could she ever recognise herself as the community of those who may have fellowship with God? It is only in Israel as her model that this is revealed to her. But in that model there is revealed to her the judgement under which she herself stands.

This judgement is of course not the only thing which is revealed to her in her model, Israel. The Old Testament speaks of the divine election, calling, preservation, increase, blessing and guidance of this evil people. It speaks—and this is its real subject —of sinful men who are possessed of a divine *promise*, and appointed to believe this promise and to live in the strength of this belief. And what is promised is that One will come to make amends for them all for the evil that they all have done, so that God may show kindness to them all and that they all may be justified and saved. The history of Israel is the history of the manifestation of this promise and of the signs which point to it. Abraham and Moses bear witness to it, as does the deliverance from Egypt and the entry into Canaan, the judges, the kings, the prophets, the Exile and the return from Exile. Each and all speak in their own particular way and their own particular place—what are called the Messianic prophecies in the Old Testament are only one of the representatives of the promise which forms the content of the whole Old Testament. Everything in the Old Testament speaks of this and says that One will come who is a descendent of Abraham and therefore a member of that people, a prophet like Moses, a priest like Aaron, a deliverer like Samson, a king like David, a sacrifice like that slain on the great day of Atonement, a representative who bears the sins of others like Jeremiah and the Servant of God in Isaiah 53, one who cries from the depths to God and is justified by God on high, like him whose voice we hear in the Psalms. It is in Him and through Him that Israel will live. It is His shadow that can be traced clearly or faintly in things great and small, everywhere in Israel's history. Israel already lives in and by the fact that He will come, and the church as she looks in the model provided by Israel, recognises that she lives by the fact that He has come and will come again.

We must not fail to understand that Israel lives by it, while all through its history refusing to live by it. Israel disobeys Moses, transgresses the law, rejects and slays the prophets, Israel does again all through its history what Adam did. It does not become gradually better, purer, more religious and more capable of being used; on the contrary, its existence is and remains a unique confirmation of human *unfaithfulness* and of the justice of the divine judgement. Israel does not believe the promise. The promise that Israel, evil in itself, shall be good in and through that one person is a promise which is proved true in advance before the coming of Christ in this respect at least, that any possibility of Israel itself making amends is clearly excluded. Whatever is in its power is done to destroy the promise. Israel rejects the promise and that in the very moment of its fulfilment. For it, Jesus, Christ can only be a blasphemer, whom it expels, delivering him over to the Gentiles as one accursed. Thus in all ages and all through its history it certainly does not live by what it itself is and does. On the contrary, when it does live, it lives by the truth of the promise that its coming prophet, priest and king will be its justification and salvation. And the model of Israel teaches the church that the faith to which she is called can only be faith in Him " Who justifieth the ungodly " (Rom. 4, 5).

But the statements of the Scottish Confession about the Old Testament require at this point to be supplemented, or rather to be qualified, if they are to be completely intelligible. We must go farther than our Confession. There is something else which the Old Testament tells us about Israel. When it testifies to Israel's unfaithfulness and the wrath of God against that unfaithfulness, it speaks of a root which survives the continual lopping off of the branches and finally the felling of the trunk itself, and of a *Remnant* of faithful and obedient believers in Israel, who are gathered together and sustained again and again. It is to be noted that their numbers are always insignificant. What are 7000 who have not bowed the knee to Baal in the midst of 100,000 people ? It is to be noted further that they themselves do not withdraw from the solidarity of the guilt of their people. On the contrary, it is they themselves who recognise it and confess it as their own personal guilt. And it is to be noted that this is no fiction. On the contrary, this remnant are actually as guilty as all the others. Is it not true that at the end, even the faithful disciples of Jesus were in the same position as Judas and Caiaphas ? So even when we consider these Few, it is just as much a miracle, when the promise lives on in their midst and is thereby preserved for the whole people. If Israel does not abide by the promise, yet the promise abides by Israel. The Remnant, the Few, are those who know this fact and hold fast to it, without their being themselves better, more believing or more upright than the others. It is on their account that the election, calling, preservation, increase, blessing and guidance of Israel does not cease to exist. In · their history above all, He Who is to come casts His shadow before Him. It is in them therefore, that Israel continues to exist despite all her unfaithfulness and despite the wrath of God which pursues it. The mountains depart and the hills are moved, but the grace of God does not depart and the covenant cannot be moved on His side. It is this by which the Few are upheld and in the Few the whole people. Because the covenant cannot fail on God's side, the existence of Israel testifies to the positive truth also of the promise given her, testifying to its *basis* and so to the *object* of the faith placed in the promise. This basis and object is He who truly comes to make amends for the evil men do. And seeing herself in her model Israel, the church recognises that in every place and age she lives in the few who, though no better than the others, cannot abandon the promise, because the promise does not abandon them, but remains with them despite the unfaithfulness of the whole to which they belong and despite their own unfaithfulness, and in and despite the judgements which are passed on the church also.

Such is the revelation of God according to the testimony of the Old Testament. It testifies to the existence of a body of men who cannot help themselves, but who receive help from Another, Who none the less comes forth from their midst to be their Head, from One against Whom they all incur guilt but Who makes amends for all their guilt. The Old Testament is a witness to Christ in so far as it makes the existence of the church of Jesus Christ manifest.

III

The witness of the New Testament can be summed up in a single sentence : " [The Sonne of God] tuke the nature of man-head." The true God, without ceasing to be the true God, has become true man. This testimony would be misunderstood if an attempt were made to say less than this on the one side or the other. We must say both true God and true man, and both must be taken in all seriousness. God has so utterly humbled Himself, that He has submitted

Himself to being in Jesus Christ what we are. And God has exalted man so highly, that the man Jesus Christ was no less than God Himself. Such is the history of Jesus Christ. It can only be understood when viewed from the standpoint of the history of Israel, which is the model of the life of the church, just as the history of Israel and the life of the church can only be understood when viewed from the standpoint of the history of Jesus Christ, on which they are founded. Israel and the church live by the truth of the promise that a member of this people, and therefore One who is Himself a *man*, will make amends for all, for what all the others fail to make amends for. But what can that mean but that *God* Himself will do this. " Who can forgive sins but God only ? " (Mark 2, 7). Moses, David, Jeremiah and the Few who form the holy Remnant were not God, but men, themselves in need of forgiveness and therefore only the shadows cast before Him by the promised One. The promise would have been vain if the promised One had not been a member of that people and not therefore a *man*. It would have been equally vain if He like all those others had only been a member of that people, and therefore only a man and not *God* Himself, and this is the testimony and the proclamation of the New Testament, that He Who is the fulfilment of the promise is not still to come, but that He *has come* already and is the fulfilment of the promise because He is true *man*, the seed of Abraham and David, an Israelite like all the others, and then as such no less than *God* Himself, Jahweh-Kyrios. Thus His history is the goal, significance and content of the history of

E 65

Israel. For that is the history of the unfaithfulness of a people, which remains only too faithful to its character by rejecting Him and having Him nailed to the Cross, but the history of Israel is much rather the history of the faithfulness of God Who in Christ cared for man, whose disobedience has now shown itself to be complete and final. Jesus Christ is the revelation of God, the same revelation as was witnessed to in the Old Testament, but the fulfilment of what in the Old Testament was witnessed to as a promise.

IV

The documents which witness to the revelation of God in Jesus Christ are the canonical Scriptures of the Old and New Testaments. It is one of the peculiarities of the *Confessio Scotica* that it does not deal with the problems which arise in this connection at the beginning of the whole work, as is usual elsewhere, but treats of them in a much later context (Art. 19-20). It is not, however, false to its spirit to insert a short note at least at this point on the *knowledge* of revelation. These documents, the canonical writings of the Old and New Testaments, are human documents. Since this is so, we are given the unavoidable task óf understanding them in a human way, and also enabled to do so. This task is performed by the scientific study of the Bible, which in recent times has developed into what is called the historical and critical study of the Bible. This is just the point where it is important for us to note that neither too little nor too much should be expected from such a study. One is entitled to expect from it that it will clarify the whole human form of the witness to Christ in the Old and New Testaments, throwing light on its linguistic, literary, historical and religious-historical aspects. But we should not expect it to set before us the object of this testimony, which is God's revelation and therefore Jesus Christ as the Messiah of Israel and the Lord of His Church. How could revelation ever be recognised as the divine content of that testimony except through revelation ? But so to recognise revelation through revelation means to recognise it by revelation awakening one's faith. To recognise that twofold history in the Bible as what it is, one must participate in it oneself, and to do so would be to have faith awakened by revelation itself. Without that, the scientific study of the Bible will certainly miss the divine content of this testimony. But in that case can it rightly clarify even its human form ? What can it see if it fails to see this twofold history ? It is to be feared that the scientific study of the Bible practised by superstition, error or unbelief will perform its task poorly in its own sphere also. How can it see the form when it does not see the content ? We may take it as true that these human documents on their human side also can only be rightly interpreted in the Church.

LECTURE VII

GOD'S DECISION AND MAN'S ELECTION

(Art. 7-8)

ART. VII

WHY IT BEHOOVED THE MEDIATOR TO BE VERY GOD AND VERY MAN

We acknawledge and confesse, that this maist wonderous conjunction betwixt the God-head and the man-head in *Christ Jesus*, did proceed from the eternall and immutable decree of God, from quhilk al our salvatioun springs and depends.

ART. VIII

OF ELECTION

For that same eternall God and Father, who of meere grace elected us in *Christ Jesus* his Sonne, befoir the foundatioun of the warld was laide, appointed him to be our Head, our Brother, our Pastor, and great Bischop of our sauls. Bot because that the enimitie betwixt the justice of God and our sins was sik, that na flesh be it selfe culd or might have attained unto God : It behooved that the Sonne of God suld descend unto us, and tak himselfe a bodie of our bodie, flesh of our flesh, and bone of our bones, and so become the Mediator betwixt God and man, giving power to so many as beleeve in him, to be the sonnes of God ; as himselfe dois witnesse, *I passe up to my Father, and unto zour Father, to my God, and unto zour God.* Be quhilk maist holie fraternitie, quhatsaever wee have tynt in *Adam*, is restored unto us agayne. And for this cause, ar we not affrayed to cal God our Father, not sa meikle because he hes created us, quhilk we have common with the reprobate ; as for that, that he hes given to us his onely Sonne, to be our brother, and

68

given unto us grace, to acknawledge and imbrace him for our
onlie Mediatour, as before is said. It behooved farther the
Messias and Redemer to be very God and very man, because
he was to underlie the punisçhment due for our transgressiouns,
and to present himselfe in the presence of his Fathers Judgment,
as in our persone, to suffer for our transgression and inobedience,
be death to overcome him that was author of death. Bot
because the only God-head culd not suffer death, neither zit
culd the onlie man-head overcome the samin, he joyned both
togither in one persone, that the imbecillitie of the ane, suld
suffer and be subject to death, quhilk we had deserved : And
the infinit and invincible power of the uther, to wit, of the
God-head, suld triumph and purchesse to us life, libertie, and
perpetuall victory : And so we confes, and maist undoubtedly
beleeve.

I

The heading of Article 8 is " of Election." But
the contents of this article seem at first sight to be
of a purely Christological character, presenting and
establishing in detail the statements of Article 4 on
the true divinity and humanity of Jesus Christ. Conversely the heading of Article 7 raises the Christological question, Cur Deus Homo ? But the answer,
which is admittedly very short, consists solely in a
reference to the divine decree, by which, the Confession says, the whole salvation of man is ordained.
Here again, as in the doctrine of sin, we are confronted
with a noteworthy innovation in the ordering of its
subject-matter on the part of the Scottish Confession.
By this arrangement its authors have made it known
unambiguously that they wish the whole body of
material which is called the *doctrine* of *Predestination*
to be explained through *Christology* and conversely

Christology to be explained through the *doctrine of Predestination.* Unfortunately they have not said *how* they wished this mutual relation to be explained, but have contented themselves with making it manifest. They have therefore presented us with a riddle and a task which we shall have to work out unaided. But we must admit, as in the case of Articles 2 and 3, that they have accomplished something significant in making manifest this relation so expressly, and that they have thereby presented us with a task which is both significant and fruitful.

If we take our authors strictly at their word in regard to what they say in Articles 7 and 8, the general view of the matter to which we attain in the first instance is as follows : Jesus Christ, true God and true man, is, as the Revelation of God, the *God* who deals with *man.* He is the *eternal* God, who deals with man and who therefore acts in *time.* He is the *just* God who deals *mercifully* with sinful man. He is the God whose action consists in His *deciding* in favour of man and in His *choosing* or *electing* man. He is the God whose action is directed by His desire to have *fellowship with man.* God's decision is accordingly what the Scottish Confession calls the decree, and " the choosing of man " is what it calls election. According to our view these two make up the one course of action which God has adopted towards men ; a course of action at once just *and* merciful, eternal *and* in time. And following the direction of the Scottish Confession the point which we make here is that the course of action which God adopts towards man is identical with the existence of Jesus Christ. The

70

existence of Jesus Christ is God's decision and man's election. This is the position which we have to develop in this lecture.

II

To know Jesus Christ is to know God, the one and only God, majestic and personal, the Creator and Lord of the world and man. To know this God in His dealings, viz. in His *decision* in favour of man, means necessarily to know God's free *mercy*, the most incomprehensible of all *miracles*. That eternity really meets us in *time*, is not a matter of course but a miracle, nor was it a matter of course that God really became *man* and has not only decided to have fellowship with us but has decided to do so in this absolute and irrevocable way, whereby He Himself became what we are. God could exist without us. He is under no debt to give Himself to us. For neither in His Divine nature does He need us, nor can any such obligation rest on Him as Creator of the world and man, still less against the background of human rebellion. Indeed we must admit that in face of human rebellion, God would *have to be against* man. Hence to know Jesus Christ is to know God in the amazement and terror expressed by such passages as : " I am not worthy of the least of all Thy mercies and of all the truth which Thou hast showed unto Thy servant " (Gen. 32, 10). " I am not worthy that Thou shouldst come under my roof " (Mt. 8, 8). " I am no more worthy to be called Thy son " (Lk. 15, 19). Though God has established fellowship between man and Himself and—let me repeat—done so in this absolute and irrevocable way whereby He Himself became what we are, yet this is something which man has not deserved, of which he is not capable and to which he can contribute nothing. But if God has thus established fellowship with man, and this is so in Jesus Christ, who is the " eternall and immutable decree of God " fully consummated—then here we stand confronted with the depths of God's goodness, which we can describe only haltingly even by the word " Grace " and all explanations of it.

But we may not stop at this point in our knowledge of Jesus Christ especially. Grace is not arbitrariness. The depths of God's goodness are not that strange abyss which we call a paradox. The divine freedom is not the whim of a tyrant, able to incline equally well in one direction or in another. God does not become unfaithful to Himself when He shows us His incomprehensible faithfulness. On the contrary, we now stand before the other side of the mystery of Jesus Christ; God is not merely merciful, He is *just* when He is merciful. God acts in accordance with His own inviolable *ordinance* when He performs miracles. While God's becoming *man* is not a matter of course, yet it can be justly considered as the most natural of all natural occurrences, because it was *God* who became man in Jesus Christ. While it is beyond our comprehension that eternity should meet us in *time*, yet it is true because in Jesus Christ *eternity* has become time. While God must be against and without man when considered as the man whom we recognise in ourselves, the creature who has fallen in sin and who, wishing to injure God's glory, has lost

his own glory besides, yet God cannot be against
and without the man, whom He Himself is in His
Son. While it would be monstrous for us to make
our human capacities and merits the ground for de-
manding that God must have fellowship with man,
yet it is perfectly normal that God should have
fellowship with man at that point, where He Himself
as man has taken man's place and where He therefore
finds Himself again in man, thus finding again in a
human life and death, real, proper and active obedience.
This is something greater and something better than
anything which God ever demanded from man or
which man could have rendered, even if he had remained sinless. It is something greater and something
better than all the prophets and all the other servants
of God have ever rendered, for it is God's own divine
perfection. And it is this that He finds again in the
man Jesus Christ—" This is my Beloved Son in Whom
I am well pleased." How should the Father be anything but well pleased with the man who is not only
what we others ought to be and are not, a clear mirror
of His glory, but who as His own beloved Son is
Himself God from eternity to eternity ? To sum up,
if God looks at man in *Jesus Christ*, then His good
pleasure in man is the strictest justice, as is His decision
to have fellowship with him, and the whole incomprehensible " Yea " which God speaks to man is the
strictest justice, just as certainly as we can only understand it as free mercy in so far as it concerns *us*. And
what if that is the case, if the meaning of this decision,
the content of that " eternall and immutable decree "
is that God will look at man in no other way than in

73

His Son Jesus Christ ? What if the Son of God has taken our place that we might come to stand in His place ? What if we might be permitted to become by grace what He is by nature ? It is this that we have to recognise as true, when we recognise Jesus Christ aright. God sees us in His beloved Son—that is the joy of the good news. Then it clearly holds good for us also, that God in being merciful to us allows nothing but the strictest justice to befall us, not on our account but for the sake of Jesus Christ in our " maist holie fraternitie " with Him. His decision to be *for* us and to call us His dear *children*, though He hates sin and tolerates no stain on His glory, is therefore one which we must accept as a valid legal ground and the holiest of ordinances.

III

In the last sentences we have assumed that to know Jesus Christ means not only to know God but also to know the *election* of man, which takes place as God *executes* His decision, and thus to know Jesus Christ means to know a new man, the elect *man*. At this point too, we are dealing with *God's* action, and let it be said at once, that God's action, when we consider it in the light of its result in man upon whom God acts, appears as free *mercy*, as a *miracle* wrought by God, no less than it did when we were dealing with its origin in God Himself. It is for this reason that Scripture and with it church-tradition speak of *election* in the case of man who is permitted to have fellowship with God, to be called and to be His child, on account of the divine decision. To be God's child is some-

74

thing which no man is by nature, or by his own strength and achievement or because of any claim which he has to be so. To be permitted to live with God and to escape perishing without Him is something which no man has chosen for himself. When man chooses he chooses the opposite. How can *God* become man, or *eternity* meet us in time? How can man come even to have part in *God*, or time come even to have a share in *eternity?* What answer can we give? But the answer is already given us: " Ye have not chosen Me, but I have chosen you " (John 15, 16). " Choosing " or " Election " means that it is so, because God wills and makes it so. By the power of God's action man *becomes* what he *cannot* be by his own strength. " Election " means " with men this is impossible, but with God all things are possible " (Mt. 19, 26). " Election " means that man is plucked like a brand from the burning out of the midst of the universal position and condition of all men by nature. We know about election because we know about Jesus Christ. *He* is the elect One, the man who is not only man but God. *He* is the miracle of Grace, in whom what is impossible for any man, is possible for man, i.e. in Him it is possible for man to have not merely a part in God but to include the fullness of Godhead in himself and be the son of God. But it is He and none other who is the *miracle* of *grace*. Once more we stand confronted by the depths of God's goodness, this time from the other side. Before it all words are hushed, and we, when we see Him, can only worship.

But once again the second step must be taken.

75

Once again grace is not arbitrariness or the whim of some dark fate. Here too God is not unfaithful to Himself, when in His election of man He keeps faith with man, who has not chosen Him. He keeps faith with us by becoming *man* and taking *our place*. But that means that He makes all our incapacity *His own*, the incapacity for which we are to blame, because it is founded on our unwillingness. Our burden, the fact that we cannot live with Him, but must perish without Him, becomes *His* burden. He Himself becomes the One Who cannot choose salvation, but can choose only the curse. He Himself bears the whole boundless affliction of this curse which lies upon us. Make no mistake, *that* is what happens when God becomes man. *That* is Jesus Christ in the suffering obedience of His life and death. He has become the one on whom the curse rests. And because God looks at man in *Jesus Christ*, His election of man to fellowship with Him, the incomprehensible " Yea " which God speaks to man is once again the strictest justice, just as certainly as we can understand it only as free mercy in so far as it concerns *us*. If it is true—and we have previously seen that it is true —that God finds Himself again in Jesus Christ, finds again His own perfection in Him and thus finds again in Him man righteous in His sight, where is then man's rejection, the guilt of his unwillingness and the curse of his expulsion ? Is what is impossible for man not, in point of fact, possible for God ? Has He not already brought this about by taking on Himself all the guilt and punishment which oppress us, bearing them, removing them, covering them up

76

and throwing them into the depths of the sea ? How could that which God Himself has borne in our stead weigh us down any longer ? Because that has happened, it is clear, that it is not merely the opportunity for our election which has been given. Because that has happened we *are* already those whose place has been taken by Jesus Christ, who has made our rejection His own, and therefore we are already the elect of God. No one and nothing can ever again tear us from His hand after He has laid it so completely and powerfully upon us. We are the chosen of God and such we are by mercy. How could we say anything else, when we look at ourselves ? But we are so also in accordance with the strictest justice. How could we say anything else when we look at Jesus Christ and ourselves in Jesus Christ, seeing that God Himself wishes to look at us in this and in no other way ?

IV

We will conclude this lecture also with certain delimitations. The Scottish Confession is right in principle in the position it takes. God's eternal decree and man's election and thus the whole of what is called the doctrine of Predestination cannot but be misunderstood unless it is understood in its connection with the truth of the divine-human nature of Jesus Christ. But the connection between these two doctrines must be considered to be even closer than the authors of the Scottish Confession presumably thought it to be, and this is just what we have tried to bring out. The word " predestination " is unfortunate in so far as by it something has been understood other than what has taken place in Jesus Christ. The treatment and proclamation of the doctrine of Predestination has all along suffered from the defect that its exponents have to a greater or less degree detached it from this connection with God's revelation in Jesus Christ. Some have sought the ultimate mystery of Predestination in a divine determination of man, which took place in some sort of eternity before and without Jesus Christ. But this eternity would be an empty one, and man would seek in vain to conceive of it as mercy and justice, whereas what was done antequam mundi iacta essent fundamenta (Eph. 1, 4) is, according to the whole New Testament, undoubtedly identical with what took place in the stable at Bethlehem and on the Cross on Calvary. Eternity is here in time. Calvin's doctrine of Predestination suffers from this error of distinguishing God's decree and the existence of Jesus Christ, and it may be conjectured that the thinking of the authors of the Scottish Confession, too, ran in this direction, despite their good beginning. I do not claim in this lecture to have propounded the doctrine of Predestination according to Calvin or the Scottish Confession. The opposite error is that of the Lutherans of the sixteenth and seventeenth centuries. These latter, because they rejected Calvin's absolute decree, sought the mystery of Predestination in man's freedom to believe and therefore in the nature of man or in a quality in him. In so doing they on their part lost sight of the free action of the God who is merciful and just. Calvin errs on the objective side, the

Lutherans on the subjective side. It must be admitted that these two solutions bear only too clearly the traces of a natural theology, the traces, that is, of a general view of the freedom of God, based on one philosophical system or another. The true mystery of Predestination is neither the secular mystery of determinism nor the equally secular mystery of indeterminism, but the holy and real mystery of Jesus Christ.

GOD'S WORK AND MAN'S SALVATION

(Art. 9-10)

ART. IX

OF CHRIST'S DEATH, PASSION, AND BURIAL

That our Lord *Jesus* offered himselfe a voluntary Sacrifice unto his Father for us, that he suffered contradiction of sinners, that he was wounded and plagued for our transgressiouns, that hee being the cleane innocent Lambe of God, was damned in the presence of an earthlie Judge, that we suld be absolved befoir the tribunal seat of our God. That hee suffered not onlie the cruell death of the Crosse, quhilk was accursed be the sentence of God; bot also that he suffered for a season the wrath of his Father, quhilk sinners had deserved. Bot zit we avow that he remained the only welbeloved and blessed Sonne of his Father, even in the middest of his anguish and torment, quhilk hee suffered in bodie and saule, to mak the full satisfaction for the sinnes of the people. After the quhilk we confesse and avow, that there remaines na uther Sacrifice for sinne, quhilk gif ony affirme, we nathing dout to avow, that they ar blasphemous against *Christs* death, and the ever-lasting purgatioun and satisfactioun purchased to us be the same.

ART. X

OF THE RESURRECTION

We undoubtedlie beleeve, that in sa mekle as it wes impossible, that the dolours of death sulde reteine in bondage the Author of life, that our LORD JESUS crucified, dead and buryed, quha descended into hell, did ryse agayne for our Justificatioun, and destroying of him quha wes the Author of death, brocht life againe to us, that wer subject to death, and to the bondage of the same. We knaw that his Resurrectioun wes confirmed be the testimonie of his verie Enemies, be the resurrectioun of the dead, quhais Sepultures did oppen, and they did ryse, and appeared to mony, within the Cittie of *Jerusalem*. It wes also confirmed be the testimonie of his Angels, and be the senses and judgements of his Apostles, and of uthers, quha had conversatioun, and did eate and drink with him, after his Resurrection.

I

In order to survey Articles 9-10, we may start with the question which we left open in the previous lecture, although there could be no doubt about the answer even there. The question is : What is the distinguishing mark of man as elected by God ? To this Articles 9-10 reply in the characteristic way hitherto adopted, by giving two answers which are to be distinguished but not separated. Both answers speak of man's *salvation*, even although this word, which sums up their content, is not expressly used. Man's salvation is his deliverance, but it is more than that. It is his restoration, but it is more than that. It is his translation to a higher status than the one which he had occupied by virtue of his creation and within the original dispensation. Salvation means therefore not merely that man is saved from certain very serious consequences of his sin, or merely that his original relation to God is restored. Beyond all this, salvation means that man becomes a new man. This new man is the man who in God's sight is not a sinner but a righteous being, and therefore one who has escaped from death and partakes of life. It is this partaking

F

of salvation which is the distinguishing mark of man as elected by God.

Even if we have only an inkling of all that this entails, it is enough to let us grasp the fact (as the contents of our previous lecture too would already lead us to expect) that the *Confessio Scotica* in this very passage says nothing whatsoever directly about man as man, as if by his own work he could accomplish his salvation or even contribute to it. We look in vain for any such view in Articles 9-10. On the contrary, in this very passage the Confession speaks exclusively of one subject, Jesus Christ, as the One in and through whom man has received his salvation (1) by being absolved from his sin in virtue of Christ's death on the cross and (2) by being proclaimed a righteous being, who is to live, in virtue of Christ's resurrection from the dead. Therefore man's salvation is not the work of man, but the work of God, and that is what is meant by the title of our lecture. The work of God, as it takes place and manifests itself in His revelation, is the incarnation of His Son, and the death and resurrection of Jesus Christ as the epitome and consummation of that incarnation.

II

The guiding conception, through which the Scottish Confession develops its view of the death of Jesus Christ, which we deal with first, is that of *sacrifice*. Jesus Christ gives Himself up not only to the power of human disorder and order, human arbitrariness and justice, but to the power of the wrath of God,

82

deservedly kindled against man. He takes the place
of sinful man and undergoes the punishment which
man was bound to undergo, in order that man may be
free and his sins forgiven, Jesus Christ is " delivered
for our offences " (Rom. 4, 25).

In order to understand this, it is necessary first to
keep before us the fact which occupied us all through
our last lecture, that God becomes *man,* As man
Jesus Christ *is able* to offer Himself as a sacrifice, and
as man He *does* so also. The death of Jesus Christ
is the sum and consummation of the incarnation of
the Son of God, in so far as His death makes it clear
that the incarnation means the humiliation—the complete humiliation of God. The picture of Jesus
Christ the Crucified reveals what the curse, the plight
and the despair of sinful man mean. Other pictures
of human suffering exist as well, pictures too of com-
paratively innocent human suffering. But it cannot
be said of any of the many others who as men have
suffered, are suffering and will suffer, that they have
endured the wrath of God. It is the suffering of
Jesus Christ utterly and alone which is " the revelation
of the wrath of God revealed from heaven " (Rom. 1,
18). Jesus Christ and He alone has experienced what
sin and death really mean. The completeness of
God's humiliation in the crucifixion of Jesus Christ
and the boundlessness of the self-sacrifice He accomplished here, lies in His taking upon Himself as man
everything which man's rebellion against Him has
made inevitable—suffering and death but also perdition and hell, punishment in time *and* in eternity,
in utter disregard of the fact that this is not worthy

83

of Him as God. Where does God remain and what still remains His, as God, when God's Son has been slain on Calvary? * It is certainly true that if ever there was a sacrifice, the death of Jesus Christ is the sacrifice of sacrifices.

But now if we are to understand this, we must remember the other fact which occupied us all through our last lecture, that it was *God* who became man and that as God Jesus Christ *is able* to make His sacrifice profitable and beneficial, and that as God He *does* so also. Even on Calvary and in the death of His Son, in the depth of this self-sacrifice and humiliation, God does not cease to be true and eternal God. For how could God cease to be God? And because He is God, He possesses the will and the power also to *accept* the sacrifice made by Himself and thus to let His own humiliation operate as *satisfaction* and to acknowledge His own bearing of man's sin, guilt and punishment as the *atonement*, which has taken place for the violation of His ordinance. Thus and for this reason He possesses the will and the power not to reckon man's sin—our sin—against him, to remember his guilt no more, and not to inflict the punishment due to him. His reason for passing it all over is that He has taken man's sin, guilt and punishment away from man and upon Himself. It is only because He is God that His infinite sacrifice can possess this infinite significance. But because He is God, this

* I have received a letter, the writer of which maintains that it is both impossible and incomprehensible that God should suffer death and perdition. To this I would reply that this is the sacrifice of which the Bible speaks. (See further note, p. 86.)

84

sacrifice can and does possess this truly infinite significance that for Jesus Christ's sake man is not a sinner and therefore also not condemned and lost but is released—for time and eternity, once for all and completely—from the bondage under which he had come. What was it that Jesus Himself said? " Thy sins are forgiven thee " (Mark 2, 5). That is the release and the acquittal granted. How could it be valid and efficacious except on the lips of God Himself against whom we have sinned? For that very reason this is the one and only acquittal. But the One against whom we have sinned, the living God, is the person from whom we receive an acquittal which is full and final because it comes from His own lips. He has humbled Himself to the uttermost in His incarnation. It is He, the same living God, who says to us in His humiliation, that on account of it our humiliation is at an end.

III

What the Scottish Confession says in Article 10 concerning the resurrection of Christ is less complete and penetrating than what it said concerning His death. It is a cause for surprise that more than half of the text of Article 10 is devoted to a kind of apologetical proof of the historical truth of the resurrection, the necessity for which is not clear. But one can recognise that the authors saw the meaning of the resurrection—which is the other side of the epitome and consummation of the incarnation of the Son of God—in the *victory* gained there by the Author of life over the author of death. The self-sacrifice of

God is proved not to have been in vain by the fact that death cannot hold Jesus Christ, who was put to death for the sake of man's sin, and that thereby man is not only acquitted but declared righteous and so has become a partaker in everlasting life. " He was raised for our justification " (Rom. 4, 25).

In distinction from what we did before, we must now begin from the fact that it was *God* who became man. It is because Jesus Christ is God, the eternal Son of the eternal Father, that death cannot hold Him and that His death can only be a gateway to life. Corresponding to the humiliation of the Son of God in His death we have the exaltation of the Son of man through His power as Son of God, a power not diminished, let alone destroyed, by His humiliation.* If He is the true God, and therefore the creator and author of all life, how could He, while yielding to the power of death, be anything but its conqueror ? But this is the very fact which Calvary renders fundamentally questionable. The Son of God in reality and not only in appearance has come under the judgement of God infinitely more deeply and really than any man whatsoever. Can it be true after all that He was not the Messiah of Israel, the Son of God ? Was He only a man like all of us, specially marked out and punished by God ? Was He, as the charge ran, a blasphemer ? The fact that He is the Lord of life with power to forgive sins, requires just as thorough-

---

* I personally could give no answer to my correspondent (see page 84), who objected that the humiliation and death of the Son of God is impossible. But here is the answer. The resurrection is the answer to the impossibility of His death.

going a proof now as did the fact of His death. The proof consists in the rising from the dead, the transfiguring and glorifying of the *man* Jesus Christ. In His unity with man the Son of God endures death; then conversely it must be in His unity with man that He conquers it. The content of the Easter message is that this has happened, that this dead man, as such, has appeared in a new life to His own people and as man is God for ever and ever. It is possible to deny and reject the Easter message, or even to say roundly that it is impossible. But the only form in which it can be affirmed and understood is to say that this man as man has arisen. Any qualification in this instance would be equivalent to a denial. For if Jesus Christ has not risen, if He has not risen as man, and therefore visibly and corporally risen from the dead, then He has not revealed Himself as the Son of God, then we know nothing about His having been so, nor do we know anything of the infinite value of His sacrifice. In that case we would have no knowledge of the forgiveness of our sin or of our election or of God's gracious decision in our favour. In that case the whole Christian church is based on an illusion and the whole of what is called Christianity is one huge piece of moral sentimentalism, to which we cannot say farewell soon enough—if Christ had not risen from the dead, then I would have no desire to stand before you as a theologian—but that all this is not so, rests entirely on the fact that Jesus Christ was God Himself. And our knowledge that this is no dream but the truth, and the fact that we have received that knowledge, rest entirely on the Easter message literally understood. It is certainly true that " if Christ be not raised, your faith is vain ; ye are yet in your sins " (1 Cor. 15, 17). And thus it is certainly true that here is the real dividing point where revelation as a whole and with it the entire Christian faith is either affirmed or denied. A confession which was weak at this point would not be a Christian confession. Whether a confession is good, bad or indifferent, is to be decided by the consistency with which it proceeds in its thought and expression from this affirmative attitude, which must be adopted towards revelation here, because revelation itself has given an affirmation at this point. Thank God that the Scottish Confession is a good confession at this point, and pray God that the Church of Scotland to-day will affirm this.

Perhaps this will be still clearer, if at this point also we start once more from the other truth that God became *man*. It is certainly not by the power of His humanity that Jesus Christ rose from the dead. There is therefore no point in asserting that a dead man could not become alive again. Naturally not, how could he ? For what the Easter message asserts is not that He was able to do so as man, by virtue of some potentiality or other present in His humanity. On the contrary, it ascribes the fact that Jesus Christ has risen from the dead entirely to His divinity. But it certainly does mean that even in His resurrection Jesus Christ did not cease to be true man. What is at stake in the resurrection of Jesus Christ is the exaltation of *man* to be a partaker in the majesty of God, the realisation of a *human* life in eternal righteous-

88

ness, innocence and blessedness, and eternal life not only for God but also now for *man*. The content of the Easter message is that He, being the same as we are, namely *man*, is God from eternity, and that message is a promise for all men, because it confers on them all—again for Jesus Christ's sake—the new robe of righteousness before God and with it eternal life. What it offers therefore is not only forgiveness of sin but something positive, righteousness; not only freedom from guilt and punishment but something positive, freedom to be God's children; not only the reduction of death to relative unimportance and comfort in the hour of death, but something positive, immortal life victorious over death. " Arise, take up thy bed and walk " (Mark 2, 9). We have now to ask once more : Would that be faith which was not faith in this promise ? What would the church have to say, if she had not this to say, if she had not the justification of sinful man to proclaim ? If people to-day assert that the church is weak and that she has nothing to say, is not the reason just that she has not the courage to say *this ?* Is she not really a true church when she truly proclaims justification and a false church when she does so falsely ? But how is she to proclaim it, if she has no promise ? How is she to proclaim salvation to man, if no salvation has come ? But how could it have come, if it had not come in the *man* Jesus Christ, risen from the dead, as the apostles proclaimed Him ? Therefore when it is viewed from this side also, we possess every reason to take the decision seriously—the Either-Or, before which we stand at this point.

IV

Let us conclude here also with a critical comment.
At the end of Article 9 the *Confessio Scotica* makes a
fierce sally against those who are not content with the
one sacrifice of Jesus Christ—a sally clearly directed
against the Roman Church. Such men are called
" Blasphemous against *Christ's* death, and the everlasting purgatioun and satisfactioun purchased to us
be the same." We will be true to the spirit of the
Confessio Scotica, if we adopt this arraignment in
regard to the whole content of Articles 9-10, and
therefore in regard to the whole of what we have
described as man's salvation. Man's salvation is the
work of God. It is therefore not the work of man.
He cannot offer the sacrifice which Jesus Christ offered,
nor can he win the victory which Jesus Christ won.
He can only receive again and again the forgiveness
effected for him once for all, and the righteousness
conferred on him once for all. He can only believe.
No performance of a cult and no moral endeavour
could take the place of this receptive faith. There is
therefore no means of attaining salvation by one's
own effort, since this is absolutely forbidden us,
according to good Reformed teaching ; because we
utter blasphemy against Jesus Christ, when we do
not allow Him to be our *only* comfort in life and in
death. Does it not now become clear why and in
what sense the *Confessio Scotica* asserts so passionately
at the very beginning : " We confesse and acknawledge'
ane onelie God " ? Confession of the one and only
God has its roots here. If this was directed in those

sixteenth-century days against the Roman Church, we can certainly repeat it to-day with this same anti-Roman tendency, but preferably not in this direction only and perhaps not in this direction primarily. It is high time to announce within the Reformation church itself with the emphasis of a new truth, that man's salvation is the work of God *exclusively*, and to say anything else is to blaspheme against Jesus Christ ; or in the words of the famous passage, Romans 3, 28, in Luther's correct translation, " We conclude that a man is justified without the works of the Law by faith alone—by faith alone."

THE KINGDOM OF GOD IN THE FUTURE AND THE PRESENT LIFE OF MAN

(Art. 11)

ART XI

OF THE ASCENSION

We nathing doubt, bot the self same bodie, quhilk was borne of the Virgine, was crucified, dead, and buried, and quhilk did rise againe, did ascend into the heavens, for the accomplishment of all thinges : Quhere in our names, and for our comfort, he hes received all power in heaven and eirth, quhere he sittes at the richt hand of the Father, inaugurate in his kingdome, Advocate and onlie Mediator for us. Quhilk glorie, honour, and prerogative, he alone amonges the brethren sal posses, till that all his Enimies be made his futestule, as that we undoubtedlie beleeve they sall be in the finall Judgment : To the Execution whereof we certainelie beleve, that the same our Lord JESUS sall visiblie returne, as that hee was sene to ascend. And then we firmely beleve, that the time of refreshing and restitutioun of all things sall cum, in samekle that thir, that fra the beginning have suffered violence, injurie, and wrang, for richteousnes sake, sal inherit that blessed immortalitie promised fra the beginning.

Bot contrariwise the stubburne, inobedient, cruell oppressours, filthie personis, idolaters, and all such sortes of unfaithfull, sal be cast in the dungeoun of utter darkenesse, where their worme sall not die, nether zit their fyre sall bee extinguished. The remembrance of quhilk day, and of the Judgement to be executed in the same, is not onelie to us ane brydle, whereby our carnal lustes are refrained, bot alswa sik inestimable comfort, that nether may the threatning of worldly Princes, nether zit the feare of temporal death and present danger, move us to renounce and forsake that blessed societie, quhilk we the members have with our Head and onelie Mediator CHRIST JESUS : Whom we confesse and avow to be the Messias promised, the onlie Head of his Kirk, our just Lawgiver, our onlie hie Priest, Advocate, and Mediator. In quhilk honoures and offices, gif man or Angell presume to intruse themself, we utterlie detest and abhorre them, as blasphemous to our Soveraigne and supreme Governour CHRIST JESUS.

I

The leading thought expressed by the Scottish Confession under the heading " of the Ascension " is the following. The Kingdom of God and thus the only valid and real sovereignty and authority over all men and over the whole world is the Kingdom of Jesus Christ. Outside the Kingdom of Jesus Christ there is no kingdom of God and therefore no kingdom at all, i.e. no valid and real sovereignty and power. To *Him* is given *all* power in Heaven and on earth. The expressions " Kingdom of God " and " Kingdom of Jesus Christ " mean the same thing. But precisely because we see the Kingdom of *Jesus Christ* in the kingdom of God, we distinguish the Kingdom of God from the kingdom of this world, i.e. from the realm of all strange and false gods, the realms of nature and spirit, fate and arbitrary power. And conversely, precisely because we see the Kingdom of *God* in the kingdom of Jesus Christ, we see in the Kingdom of Jesus Christ the one single and real power over us and over all things, beside which there is no other about which we need trouble. In the light of this we can understand here once more the emphasis with which Reformed teaching speaks of the unique nature of God. But now we can understand also that it was necessary to have the name of Jesus, Christ immediately and categorically in connection with all that we said in lectures 3 and 4 about the majesty and personality of God and the creation and government of the world, and equally necessary to say whatever was said only with Him as our starting point, so to speak.

Note the strong emphasis contained in the words " the self same bodie " with which the 11th Article begins. Hence by Jesus Christ is to be understood the real *man* Jesus Christ, the same man whose revelation, true divinity and manhood, death and resurrection for our salvation had been spoken of in Articles 4-10. That it is He who is the Lord over us and over all things is unquestionably good Reformed teaching, and is to be expounded in Article 11.

II

Jesus Christ is Κύριος. What does that mean ? It means that He is *the* great *change* in man's life. He changes it radically, because He changes it in its relation to God, because His work is the salvation of man and because this work of His is the work of God Himself. There is no greater or more radical change of man's life than that which consists in the translating of man's life out of the rebellion of sin and the disaster consequent upon it into that new gratitude for his salvation which binds man once and for all and into the knowledge of the divine power of this divine work which has taken place for man and on him ; and it

94

consists in man's having the right in this gratitude and knowledge o understand his existence anew as grace and favour.

Jesus Christ is this change in man's life. And that means that it is a *hidden* change. We think of the words " Your life is hid with Christ in God " (Col. 3, 3). If it is a visible life—and how else could it be a human life ?—and if in this visible life there can be no lack of visible change of every kind, yet none of the visible changes in our life is *the* change, the *great* change which has taken place for us and on us in our relation to. God. Jesus Christ is the great change and to seek this change even for a moment elsewhere than in Him, and hence to desire to see the change instead of believing it, is to confound two things and to deceive oneself, and by this one's salvation can be lost. But this fact that Jesus Christ is the great change in the life of man means also that it is a *real* change. God's decision and man's election, the death of Jesus Christ and the forgiveness of our sins, His resurrection and our justification—all this, as we have already seen, is beyond question irrevocable and cannot be undone, because it is God who acts here. If we seek the change in our life, where we can *see* changes and hence somewhere else than in Jesus Christ, we shall certainly find it to be a very changeable kind of change ! But if we seek it in *Jesus Christ*, and hence if we seek it by believing in Him, then we find it to be a change which we can no more go back on than God can cease to be God. The hiddenness of this change of life is therefore not to be separated from its reality nor its reality from its hiddenness.

95

The *reality* of this change is proved true by its
determining man's *future* and by the way in which it
does so. What does it mean to exist as man? It
means to have a future before us. We live to-day
for to-morrow. If there were no Jesus Christ and
therefore no great change in our life, to-morrow could
not but mean the end of what we to-day are wishing,
willing and striving after. But what we wish, will
and strive after to-day, i.e. what we are to-day, is
simply our sin, which is forgiven by Jesus Christ. The
end of our sin, of our effort to-day, which could only
be death, cannot be our " to-morrow " in Jesus Christ
and in the change accomplished by Him in our lives.
Its place is taken instead by the eternal life following
on our righteousness before God which is founded on
Jesus Christ. But because it is He alone, in whom the
old end, death, is removed and a new one, eternal life,
established, we must say, " *He* is our end, our future,
and our to-morrow." I do not know who or what I
will be to-morrow. *He* has to decide about that.
Therein lies the hiddenness of my future destiny.
That points me to the fact that I must go to meet the
future in *faith* and that I can only do so in faith. But
I know that Jesus Christ will be to-morrow and
eternally—that is the reality of my future destiny
and means that I am free to *go to meet* my future in
faith.

The *hiddenness* of Christ's great change is proved
true by its determining man's *present* and by the way
in which it does so. To exist as man means to live
for to-day and not merely for to-morrow. We live
to-day for to-morrow. If it were not for Jesus Christ

and this great change, "to-day" could not but mean the very doubtful enjoyment of what we yesterday wished for, willed and sought after, the tragic harvest of what we sowed yesterday. But we sinned yesterday and this our sin of yesterday also is forgiven us in Jesus Christ. What appears in its place to-day is our righteousness before God which is founded on Jesus Christ and is valid retrospectively and for yesterday, but is none the less ours to-day. It is the new garment, and clothed with it, we, who are not Jesus Christ, may wait for Him and so may look *towards* Him as our future and hasten *towards* Him. I know that He is my full salvation—this is the reality of my present state and allows me to believe already to-day and to be joyful in faith. But who and what am I? He alone has to decide about that. This is the hiddenness of my present state which compels and obliges me still to-day to have faith and therefore to leave to Him the revelation of what to-day remains hidden.

III

He who has already come as the Messiah of Israel and done once and for all everything necessary for the salvation of man is—and is as such—the Lord of man's *future* too. He is the guarantor of our righteousness who is to come, and the bringer of eternal life whom we expect. It is therefore He who will decide who and what we shall be to-morrow and who and what we shall be finally and for all eternity. He therefore is the *Judge* with whom it rests to set men on His right hand or on His left as partaking or

G   97

not partaking in the salvation ordained in Him. The *Confessio Scotica* has spoken very clearly and concretely about this judgement of Jesus Christ and the discipline and comfort which it means for those who expect it. But the following points must be noted : (1) The Confession describes this judgement as the " refreshing and restitutioun," i.e. the restoration and manifestation of a relation which had already existed before this judgement. (2) Those who are rejected by Jesus Christ are described as " stubburne, inobedient, cruell oppressours, filthie personis, idolaters," and therefore apparently—but only apparently —in moral terms, whereas those who are accepted by Jesus Christ and partake of eternal life are not described as good, righteous, pious, etc., but simply as those " that have suffered violence, injurie and wrang." (3) In this 11th Article what is emphasised is not what we should do to prepare for this judgement, but the Being and Work of Jesus Christ as that of our advocate, mediator, priest, lawgiver and governor. All that requires us to understand in a quite specific way what our text conceives as the decision which is to be expected in Jesus Christ, i.e. what it conceives His office as Judge to be. What we have here is not just the usual view which people hold about the Last Judgement. In the judgement of Jesus Christ which we must all go to meet, it is not a question of establishing that some are righteous and the others sinners. In God's decision and man's election and in the death and resurrection of Jesus Christ it has already been decided that in ourselves and by ourselves we are *all* sinners, but that being saved through the complete incarnation of the Son of God we are *all* righteous. What is therefore involved in the expectation of Jesus Christ as the coming judge is not that I go to face this judge in fear and trembling, but that, according to the unsurpassable formulation of the Heidelberg Catechism (Q. 52), " In all my sorrows and persecutions, with uplifted head, I look for the judge, who has before offered Himself for me to the judgement of God, and removed me from all curse, to come again from heaven.", In face of this judgement there can be only one question, namely Do I really look *for Him?* Do I *believe* that He is my only and my complete salvation ? That and that alone is what will be decided at the Judgement. If I believe, then it is this life and faith of mine which will be disclosed and judged as my eternally holy and blessed life in God's light. It will be so disclosed and judged not because it is a noble faith but because it is faith in *Him.* And this after it has been in my own eyes and that of others no triumphant life, but, as the Confession describes it, one which has been worsted in its struggle with the powers of darkness in the world, a life wretched and burdensome. If I lack faith, and have sought my salvation elsewhere than in Jesus Christ, if in insolence and disobedience I have sought to perfect it myself in this way or in that one, if my " to-morrow " and ultimately my eternity has continued to be the end which I have wished for, willed and striven after—in that case how can my life be disclosed and judged as anything but a continuing in sin and therefore in the darkness of eternal death ? Note therefore that the Scottish Confession speaks

even of the judgement of Jesus Christ only in order
to repeat that He and He alone is the Saviour of man,
that men may be summoned thereby once more to
faith in Him. We are *on our way* to meet this judgement, there is therefore point in summoning us to
faith ; for we have still time to believe. And *He
Himself* is the judge, He who wills that all men be suc-
coured and who acknowledges our sin only as forgiven
sin and our condemnation only as the condemnation
borne by Him. We have therefore not merely time
but also *ground* and *occasion* for believing. Jesus
Christ is our *Hope*, our real and certain hope. Only
if we were to set our hope not in Him but in *something
else*, could the future be one which we would have to
contemplate with *fear*.

IV

It is precisely because Jesus Christ is our future that
He also necessarily determines our *present*. To expect
Him as our judge means to believe in Him *to-day* and
therefore to acknowledge Him as our righteousness
and our life. That is the comfort of the believer and
the comfort of the church struggling and suffering in
the present. Since we have not to fear Jesus Christ
and therefore not to fear the Lord of all men and the
world, there is *no* man and *no* thing which we need
fear. What man could have power enough, or what
danger could be great enough, or how could bodily
death itself be terrible enough to frighten the man who
looks towards Jesus Christ not in fear but " with
uplifted head " ? Faith's present being completely

hidden yet completely real is a present full of joy. Faith has nothing to fear. The only thing which it could fear is that it might cease to be faith and degenerate into unbelief, error or superstition. All false belief is characterised by its deceiving men with other hopes outside and alongside Jesus Christ, and by the man who has such false faith holding fast to such other hopes. But however great and noble such hopes may be, they cause man to lose fellowship with his Saviour and to fall back into sin and under its curse. Such a man will now of necessity *fear* Jesus Christ and will now have to live his life once more in the world and among men as one afraid. The present of all false faith is a joyless present, perhaps again in a hidden sense but certainly in a real one, just as certainly as its future is darkness. It does not lie in the power of faith to maintain and sustain itself as faith. This again would be false faith wishing to live by its own powers. But true faith lives from the power of Jesus Christ Himself and on that account need not fear either that it may become false faith.

FREEDOM TO BELIEVE

(Art. 12)

ART. XII

OF FAITH IN THE HOLY GOSTE

This our Faith and the assurance of the same proceeds not fra flesh
and blude, that is to say, fra na natural poweris within us, bot
is the inspiration of the holy Gost : Whome we confesse GOD
equall with the Father and with his Sonne, quha sanctifyis
us, and bringis us in al veritie be his awin operation, without
whome we sulde remaine for ever enimies to God, and ignorant
of his Sonne *Christ Jesus ;* for of nature we are so dead, so blind,
and so perverse, that nether can we feill when we are pricked,
see the licht when it shines, nor assent to the will of God when
it is reveiled, unles the Spirit of the Lord *Jesus* quicken that
quhilk is dead, remove the darknesse from our myndes, and
bowe our stubburne hearts to the obedience of his blessed will.
And so as we confesse, that God the Father created us, when
we were not, as his Sonne our Lord *Jesus* redeemed us, when
wee were enimies to him ; so also do we confesse that the holy
Gost doth sanctifie and regenerat us, without all respect of
ony merite proceeding from us, be it before, or be it after our
Regeneration. To speak this ane thing zit in mair plaine
words : As we willingly spoyle our selves of all honour and
gloir of our awin Creation and Redemption, so do we also of
our Regeneration and Sanctification, for of our selves we ar
not sufficient to think one gude thocht, bot he quha hes begun
the wark in us, is onlie he that continewis us in the same, to
the praise and glorie of his undeserved grace.

I

We have come to the end of the first part of our lectures, and at the same time have reached the real centre of the Scottish Confession, the transition from the problems relating to the *knowledge of God* to those relating to the *service of God*. Article 12 shows us how these two, the knowledge of God and the service of God, not only belong together, but like two concentric circles with a common radius coincide. Nothing could be more foreign to the teaching of the Reformation than the idea of a knowledge of God which was not also in itself service of God, or a service of God which consisted in something else than knowledge of God. It is in this unity that they meet us in Article 12, in which besides all that has gone before is summed up and brought to its conclusion.

In accordance with what we have already heard, what do we mean by knowing God ? It has become clear that it is not a matter here of observing, analysing, considering and judging an object, where the knower is permitted to consider himself disinterested, free and superior in his relation to his object. Knowledge of God, according to the teaching of the Reformation, consists, as we have seen, in the knowledge of the God who deals with man in His Revelation in Jesus Christ. Knowledge of God according to the teaching of the Reformation does not therefore permit the man who knows to withdraw himself from God, so to speak, and to maintain an independent and secure position over against God so that from this he may form thoughts about God, which are in varying degrees true, beautiful and good. This latter procedure is that of all natural theology. One can only choose between this and the procedure of Reformed theology, one cannot reconcile them. Knowledge of God according to the teaching of the Reformation is *obedience* to God and therefore itself already service of God. According to Reformed teaching the knowledge of God is brought about when the object reaches out and grasps the subject, and through this the latter, the man who knows becomes a *new* man. All thoughts which he forms about God can only be an echo of what was said to him through God's dealing with him, by means of which he became this new man.

But the new character which man possesses through the knowledge of God consists in his having *faith*. To have faith means to allow to God, the world and ourselves true and real existence of the kind declared and laid down for us through the action of God in Jesus Christ in the past, in the present and in the future. To have faith means to live as a man who is faced by Jesus Christ. Such a man is therefore faced by the prophet who can tell us the first thing and the last thing that we have to know in order to be able to live and die. He is faced by the priest who has made amends, does and will make amends for everything. And he is faced by the king, who possesses not only the will to do this but also the power, namely the omnipotence of God. To have faith means to serve this Lord. That is why knowledge of God is nothing else than service of God.

II

Who then has faith ? How can anyone have faith ?
How does anyone come to have faith ? On this
question the *Confessio Scotica* expresses itself in the
first instance *negatively*. " This our Faith and the
assurance of the same, proceeds not fra flesh and
blude, that is to say, fra na natural poweris within us,
bot is the inspiration of the holy Gost." Note that
this answer holds good for everything that we have
become acquainted with so far as Reformed teaching
on the knowledge of God, and it will hold good also
for everything that we will become acquainted with
next year as Reformed teaching on the service of God.

If faith is the life of the man who faces Christ as
the one from Whom alone he receives his salvation,
then it is easy to understand that the man who lives
in faith, when he is confronted by the faithfulness of
God, sees himself convicted of his own unfaithfulness,
—a truth developed in the fifth lecture. Such a man
will see that he is in no position to have faith in himself, or to ascribe to himself a capacity or power by
means of which he himself could somehow bring about
his salvation, or co-operate in bringing it about.
What proceeds from himself, the man who believes
can only consider as the sin which is forgiven him.
If he were to any extent to rely on himself too, as well
as on Jesus Christ, he would to that extent fall back
into sin, and deny the completeness of the salvation
received through Jesus Christ and thus the glory of
Jesus Christ as the only Saviour. But if he cannot
rely on himself, he cannot rely on his own faith as a

work, to accomplish which he possesses the organs
and the capabilities in himself. That man is more or
less religiously inclined—if it is true—may well be a
good thing. But the man who really has faith will
never consider his faith as a realisation or manifestation of his religious life, but will on the contrary
admit that his capacity for religion would in itself have
led him to the gods and idols, but by no means to
Jesus Christ. The man who really has faith knows
the truth of the sentence of the Confession quoted
above, that it is impossible for him by his own efforts
to have faith. It is only those who do not possess
faith, who always imagine that faith is a human
potentiality, which they will probably say happens to
have been denied them personally. And the would-be
possessors of faith also, who disagree with the Confession's negative statement, and who see in their own
faith the realisation of a human potentiality, are really
not possessed of faith. Faith is not an art, nor is it
an achievement. Faith is not a good work of which
some may boast, while the others with a shrug of their
shoulders can excuse themselves by saying that they
have not the capacity for it. With faith itself comes
the conclusive insight, that no one has the capacity
for faith by his own effort, that is either the capacity
to prepare for faith or to start it, or to persevere in
it, or to perfect it. The man who has faith will understand the man who does not possess it, the sceptic
or the atheist, better in this respect than they will
understand themselves. For he will consider this
incapacity for faith not merely to be accidental, as
does the non-believer, but he will consider it to be

inevitable. Let us hear the Confession itself. " For of nature we are so dead, so blind and so perverse, that nether can we feill when we ar pricked, see the licht when it shines, nor assent to the will of God when it is reveiled." We have as little share in our rebirth, as we have in our being created or as we have in what Jesus Christ has done for us. " For of our selves we ar not sufficient to think one gude thocht. . . ." That is a hard saying, but note that it is not unbelief but faith that speaks in this way. Unbelief has, at all times, spoken quite differently.

III

Let us ask once more, who then has faith, who can have faith, who can come to have faith ? The *positive* answer given at this point by the Scottish Confession in common with all Reformed Confessions is a simple answer, and our answer, too, can be a very simple one. Everyone comes to have faith, *can* have faith, and *has* faith who does not try to evade the action of God in His revelation in Jesus Christ, but stands firm, and therefore receives the salvation effected through Jesus Christ as a *divine* salvation and also as the salvation specially appointed for *him.* Whoever does that, possesses—*by doing it*—also the freedom, the opportunity and the capacity to do it. Is it his own freedom—a freedom that he already possessed before he did this ? Is it a freedom which, so to speak, he brought with him, and has now simply applied in making the decision to believe instead of not to believe —just like the freedom by virtue of which we can decide to cross to the right instead of to the left hand side of the street ? Is it therefore a freedom which belongs to the human mind ? No-one who really believes has yet understood and described his freedom to believe as a freedom which he possessed before, and brought with him. On the contrary, by receiving what he was permitted to receive from Jesus Christ, he confessed and acknowledged that *the fact that* he did receive (instead of refusing to receive) was itself the receiving of a divine gift—God's faithfulness reaching over and grasping him, and in this he, who found in himself nothing but unfaithfulness, could only see an undeserved act of kindness and an incomprehensible miracle. Was it then a spell, a piece of magic or a marvel ? No, *he* really did receive here, while in possession of his mind, understanding, will and all his five senses. He was not an extraordinary sort of man, and it was nothing extraordinary which happened when he believed instead of not believing. It was in itself nothing more out of the ordinary than if he had crossed from the left to the right hand side of the street. He was not passive. On the contrary, he acted. He made no sacrificium intellectus. On the contrary, he thought, and that, it is to be hoped, as rigorously and consistently as it is possible for a man to think. It was not a matter of putting the intellect to sleep. He sank into no mystic trance. On the contrary, he was as wide awake and as sober as it is possible to be. And what of his religious nature ? He probably manifested too his capacity for religion ! In short, everything came about in a perfectly human way. He was no stone or log, to which something had happened without his knowing or willing it, but on the contrary he made a decision, in the way in which men are accustomed to make decisions. So hidden was the real change of life which took place in him, when it really came about that he believed instead of not believing. But *the fact that* he did come to this decision, *that* he really believed and *that* he actually had freedom to enter this new life of obedience and hope—all this was not the work of *his* spirit, but the work of the *Holy* Spirit. No one who has really had faith, has understood his faith in any other way. And the whole of Scripture bears us witness that it is impossible to understand faith in any other way. The possibility of faith becomes manifest in its actuality, but it is in its actuality that it becomes manifest as a *divine* possibility. Can God be known? Yes, God *can* be known, but God can only be known through Himself, through His revelation and through the awakening of faith in His revelation, through His eternal Word, which has become flesh, and through His Holy Spirit, which brings hearts of stone to life. In tuo lumine videbimus lumen—in thy light we shall see light (Ps. 36, 9). That is the first and the final word of Reformed teaching on the knowledge of God.

PART II

THE SERVICE OF GOD

THE REAL CHRISTIAN LIFE

(Art. 13)

ART. XIII

OF THE CAUSE OF GUDE WARKIS

Sa that the cause of gude warkis, we confesse to be not our free wil, bot the Spirit of the Lord *Jesus*, who dwelling in our hearts be trewe faith, bringis furth sik warkis, as God hes prepared for us to walke in. For this wee maist boldelie affirme, that blasphemy it is to say, that *Christ* abydes in the heartes of sik, as in whome there is no spirite of sanctification. And therefore we feir not to affirme, that murtherers, oppressers, cruell persecuters, adulterers, huremongers, filthy persouns, Idolaters, drunkards, thieves, and al workers of iniquity, have nether trew faith, nether ony portion of the Spirit of the Lord JESUS, so long as obstinatlie they continew in their wickednes. For how soone that ever the Spirit of the Lord JESUS, quhilk Gods elect children receive be trew faith, taks possession in the heart of ony man, so soone dois he regenerate and renew the same man. So that he beginnis to hait that quhilk before he loved, and begins to love that quhilk befoir he hated ; and fra thine cummis that continuall battell, quhilk is betwixt the flesh and the Spirit in Gods children, till the flesh and natural man, according to the awin corruption, lustes for things pleisand and delectable unto the self, and grudges in adversity, is lyfted up in prosperity, and at every moment is prone and reddie to offend the majestie of God. Bot the spirite of God, quhilk gives witnessing to our spirite, that we are the sonnes of God, makis us to resist filthie plesures, and to groane in Gods presence, for deliverance fra this bondage of corruption ; and finally to triumph over sin, that it reygne not in our mortal bodyis. This battell hes not the carnal men, being destitute of Gods

H   113

Spirite, bot dois followe and obey sinne with greedines, and
without repentance, even as the Devill, and their corrupt
lustes do prick them. Bot the sonnes of God, as before wes
said, dois fecht against sinne; dois sob and murne, when
they perceive themselves tempted in iniquitie; and gif they
fal, they rise againe with earnest and unfained repentance:
And thir thingis they do not be their awin power, bot be the
power of the Lord *Jesus*, without whom they were able to do
nothing.

I

The task which lies before us in this second half of
our lectures is as follows : to understand as *the true*
service of God exactly what we became familiar with
last year, under the guidance of the Scottish Confession, as *the true knowledge of God*, i.e. to understand
Christian truth as identical with Christian life. Permit
me to begin by repeating explicitly some of the most
important sentences from our last lecture. According
to Reformed teaching the knowledge of God and the
Service of God do not merely belong together, but
like two concentric circles with a common radius,
they are one. Knowledge of God is obedience to
God. Such knowledge becomes actual by man's
becoming a new man through faith in Jesus Christ
as his Lord. This newness, or, as we may say, faith,
consists in man's relying upon his Lord and not upon
himself any longer, and in his serving his Lord and
not himself any longer, and this in the freedom of
the Holy Spirit who awakens him to this obedience,
and not in any freedom of his own. Thus the true
knowledge of God is already itself service of God
and the true service of God can only consist in the

true knowledge of God. In tuo lumine videbimus lumen. Seen from this standpoint we can immediately understand the significance of the twofold delimitation and polemic with which the 13th Article of the Scottish Confession begins.

The Confession directs its attack in the first instance against the error, according to which the believer is free and able himself to decide to do good, to serve God and hence to live the Christian life. It attacks, that is to say, the error according to which knowledge of God is a theory, the contemplation of an object which imposes no obligation and does not affect our existence, a theory which must then be followed by practice, by the service of God as a matter for our own determining and willing. This opinion can only win a footing because of a failure on the part of faith to understand its own nature. Where God is truly known, man ceases to be lord over himself and his determining and willing take place no longer through his own freedom but in the freedom of the Holy Spirit. Hence there can be no question here of a special service of God which man himself must subsequently choose and perform. There is no service of God beyond and beside the knowledge of God.

The Confession directs its attacks, secondly, against the error according to which man can have faith without thereby doing what is good, serving God and hence living the Christian life. The error here attacked is fundamentally identical with the previous one. Note the " for this " with which the second sentence of our text begins. If the knowledge of God were a theory which must subsequently be followed by practice committed into human hands, the question arises why should this subsequent practice be the practice of " good works " ? Why should it not equally well and infinitely more probably take the form of practice of some self-chosen and arbitrary kind which being arbitrary would certainly be evil ? Once again the opinion that this is possible, that the knowledge of God is conceivable apart from the service of God, can only rest upon a failure of faith to understand its own nature. To repeat, where God is truly known, man ceases to be lord over himself and becomes a being who is himself sanctified through the Holy Spirit in whose freedom his determining and willing take place. There can therefore be no knowledge of God such as is not itself and as such service of God.

It is the life of the real man which gains a thoroughly definite meaning through this double delimitation— our life within the bounds of the time allotted to us by the goodness of God. This life can in no sense, good or bad, be lived in a manner arbitrarily chosen by ourselves, whether this arbitrary choice take the form of piety or of wickedness. It can and may and should be lived in faith, in the service of God which is none other than the knowledge of God, in the knowledge of God which is itself the service of God. To that end time is allotted to us and for this reason we have life. " The just shall live by faith " (Rom. 1, 17).

II

The Scottish Confession describes the new life of faith and consequently the sanctification of man by the Holy Spirit as a radical change in the nature of the objects towards which his affections of love and hate are directed. Man begins, says the Confession, " to hait that quhilk before he loved, and begins to love that quhilk befoir he hated." That is a sober realistic description. We recognise immediately that man in becoming a Christian and entering the service of God has not thereby become an angel. He lives in the world and the world lives in him. He lives under ordinances and conditions and in conformity with manners and customs which are determined and given their character not by God but by revolt against God. Man himself in his whole being and action is a partaker in this revolt. He comes to know this in the manifest imperfection of his actions and in their questionable and dangerous nature. He will find himself at all times accused and condemned by the Word of God. He is no better than the others who do not believe. Like them he is a sinner and is distinguished from them only by the fact that he is beginning to love what he previously hated and to hate what he previously loved.

What is meant by " to love what we previously hated " ? Previously, " before," means : when we were without faith and therefore without the know-ledge that God in Jesus Christ has graciously inter-vened on our behalf, that He Himself might make amends for the evil that we do. When we are without this knowledge, we hate to have a Lord and hate everything that could remind us of Him and of the fact that we ought to serve Him. The Heidelberg Catechism (Quest. 5) has expressed this with almost unbearable severity, " I am by nature inclined to hate God and my neighbour," but the configuration of human life in matters great and small goes to show, and the Word of God tells us, that this is only too true. No education and no morality can alter this in any way. I am by nature inclined to hate God and my neighbour. But in the light of the knowledge of the grace of God we begin to love what we previously hated, because He is the Lord who first loved us, loved us when we still hated Him and were yet His enemies (Rom. 5, 10). When He becomes known to us in this love of His—and faith means that He does become known to us in this love of His—then we begin to be glad to have a Lord, namely this Lord, and to be glad to have everything which reminds us of Him and of the fact that we may serve Him. We must no longer own allegiance to our sin but we are free to own allegiance to the forgiving grace of God.

And what is meant by " to hate what we previously loved " ? Previously we loved to be lords and to exercise lordship over ourselves and others, over things and ideas and even over God, or over what we took to be God. That is the love, the eros, which corresponds to the hate mentioned above. Plato was right when he described it as the most powerful of all the divinities in this world. Without the knowledge of the grace of God we shall be unable to love in any other way than this, or to love anything other than power, our own power. But in the light of this knowledge when Jesus Christ has made His Lordship and power dear to us, we begin to hate what we previously loved. We begin then to see the falsehood, the confusion, the strife and the death which that former love, the eros, has as its consequences. We begin to be terrified of our own power and of its capabilities. We let ourselves be told by the Word of God that our own power is evil. We would be glad to be rid of it. No practical philosophy will instil into us the power to hate what we by nature love with all our heart. But when Jesus Christ becomes known to us in faith as God Himself, who has given Himself for us, we begin to hate what we previously loved. To repeat, we must now own allegiance no longer to our sin but are now free to own allegiance to the grace which forgives it.

When we speak of the new life of faith, the sanctified Christian life, we are in the first instance concerned only with this change in our love and hatred, and it is of this change alone that the Confession speaks. And note that the Confession is sober and realistic in this respect also, that it speaks only of the *beginning* of this new loving and hating. The old love and the old hatred are still in action. They will continue in action in every human life right up to the end and in such a manner that one will never be able to speak of anything more than the *beginning* of new love and new hate. But this beginning, as a beginning, the fact of this change in the object of our affections, is decisive, be it even so small and weak to the very end. For though it is no total change, but probably only a minimum, yet it is a radical change in the object `of our affections. It is the sign that the new life of faith has begun. How could we have faith without our faith itself signifying at once the existence of this change.

III

We shall not have the right to see in this change in our loving and hating more than a sign. And this is equally true of the conflict with ourselves, in which the change involves us. If we were asked whether our new love and new hatred were strong enough or whether we were successful in this conflict or simply whether we were struggling seriously enough, which of us could stand this test ? Who in that case could call himself a Christian or who would have the right to do so ? But that is not what we are asked. We are asked about our faith, and when we begin in faith to have new love and new hatred, here again we shall not look in our faith to our new love and hatred for help or salvation. So too, in the conflict with ourselves we shall as little look for help or salvation to the struggle which we are putting up, whether it be good or bad, victorious or unsuccessful, serious or half-hearted. On the contrary, when we have faith, we shall have the right to see in this change and in the conflict bound up with it only a sign—the sign of a crisis divine and not human, which has overtaken our existence. We may certainly see a sign of this salutary crisis in the change and conflict. " This battell," says the Confession, " hes not the carnal men, being destitute of God's Spirite, . . . Bot the

sonnes of God dois fecht against sinne; dois sob
and murne, when they perceive themselves tempted
in iniquitie." But what helps and saves us is not this
battle which we wage, but the battle which Jesus Christ
has fought and in which He has already been victorious.
And it is about this latter we are asked, when enquiry
is made about our sanctification and our real Christian
life and consequently about our faith. We are asked,
namely, if Jesus Christ stands before us as the person
He really is, and if we recognise and acknowledge Him
as such. When that comes about, then there comes
about the thing which helps and saves us and which
makes our life in reality a Christian life and our works
good works. What happens is this, man is found
guilty of his sin, but also and to a far greater extent
is assured of the grace of God. When this happens
repeatedly and when it becomes true in our case that
Jesus Christ has borne the wrath of God for us too,
and has revealed God's love toward us, and when we
continue to accept the fact that He has done this for
us and on our behalf, and when through the daily
decisions of our lives it is decided that this is what
happens daily, and when we give God the glory by
this being the meaning and content of our daily decisions, then we are involved in the real struggle of
the Spirit, i.e. of the Holy Spirit, against the flesh,
i.e. against ourselves in the totality of our existence,
in our piety as well as in our godlessness. For this
existence of ours is what the Bible calls flesh. We
are involved in the struggle, which is also the true and
effective struggle of God on our behalf. That we
are the scene and the witnesses of this struggle is

what constitutes the real Christian life, which is a
life in which God intervenes on man's behalf. That
other struggle which we have to carry on ourselves
can be a sign but only a sign of this one, and so too
the change in our love and hatred, which necessitates
our personal struggle, can be such a sign, but only
a sign.

IV

We can now understand why the description of
sanctification in the Scottish Confession ends with a
reference to *repentance*. Repentance in the Biblical
sense of the term is the turning back to God as the
one and only helper and Saviour, in whose presence,
i.e. in the presence of whose mercy, we shall always
feel nothing but penitence, as we recall all we should
like and are able to do for ourselves. By showing
such repentance, our actions become good actions.
We are not unfaithful to our text and we are certainly
not unfaithful to Holy Scripture, if we add that here
we are concerned with *daily* repentance, with that
turning from all our own works to Jesus Christ, which
must repeatedly occur. " gif they fal," says the
Confession, Christians may and should show repentance. " If they fall "—but we all fall every day.
Seen from God's side our life is a continuous falling
and therefore our repentance must also be a daily one.
And it is just as legitimate to put *thankfulness* before
repentance, because we thereby make clear what true
repentance is. The Confession itself says expressly
that the true and unfeigned repentance of the Christian
only comes about through the power of our Lord Jesus

Christ. In fact how would it be possible for us to come to Him daily except by His daily coming to us —and that is the work of the Holy Spirit? But if He does come to us, that through His own power He may lead us to repentance, i.e. may lead us away from our own works to Himself, as the one through whom everything had to happen for our good, how in that case can thankfulness be other than the first and decisive word by which we must describe our sanctification and therefore all good action and Christian living. To be sanctified, good, Christian, means to be thankful. We have not deserved His continual coming to us through the Holy Spirit that we might come to Him anew. We have every day deserved that He should come to us no more the next day. But if He comes for all that—and we have the promise He has given to His Church, " Lo I am with you alway " (Mt. 28, 20), then our repentance and thus our real Christian life will have not merely to end with thankfulness but always to begin with it. Thankfulness is the first, not merely the last, word in the Christian life.

THE ORDINANCE GOVERNING THE CHRISTIAN LIFE

(Art. 14)

ART. XIV

WHAT WARKIS ARE REPUTIT GUDE BEFOIR GOD

We confesse and acknawledge, that God hes given to man his holy
Law, in quhilk not only ar forbidden all sik warkes as displeis
and offend his godly Majestie, but alswa ar commanded al sik
as pleis him, and as he hes promised to rewaird. And thir
warkes be of twa sortes. The ane are done to the honour of
God, the uther to the profite of our Nichtbouris ; and both
have the reveiled will of God for their assurance. To have
ane God, to worschip and honour him, to call upon him in all
our troubles, reverence his holy name, to heare his word, to
beleve the same, to communicate with his holy Sacraments,
are the warkes of the first Tabill. To honour Father, Mother,
Princes, Rulers, and superiour powers ; to love them, to support
them, zea to obey their charges (not repugning to the com-
maundment of God), to save the lives of innocents, to represse
tyrannie, to defend the oppressed, to keepe our bodies cleane
and halie, to live in sobernes and temperance, to deall justlie
with all men both in word and deed ; and finally, to represse
all appetite of our Nichbouris hurt, are the gude warkes of the
secund Tabill, quhilk are maist pleising and acceptabill unto
God, as thir warkes that are commanded be himselfe. The
contrary quhairof is sinne maist odious, quhilk alwayes displeisis
him, and provokes him to anger : As not to call upon him alone,
when we have need ; not to hear his word with reverence, to
contemne and despise it ; to have or worschip idols, to maintene
and defend Idolatrie ; lichtlie to esteeme the reverend name

of God ; to prophane, abuse, or contemne the Sacraments of *Christ Jesus ;* to disobey or resist ony that God hes placed in authoritie (quhil they passe not over the bounds of their office) ; to murther, or to consent thereto, to beare hatred, or to let innocent blude bee sched, gif wee may withstand it. And finally, the transgression of ony uther commandement in the first or secund Tabill, we confesse and affirme to be sinne, by the quhilk Gods anger and displesure is kindled against the proud unthankfull warld. So that gude warkes we affirme to be thir onlie, that are done in faith, and at Gods command-ment, quha in his Lawe hes expressed what the thingis be that pleis him. And evill warkis we affirme not only thir that expressedly ar done against Gods commaundement : bot thir alswa that in matteris of Religioùn, and worschipping of God, hes na uther assurance bot the inventioun and opinioun of man : quhilk God fra the beginning hes ever rejected, as be the Prophet *Esay*, and be our Maister CHRIST JESUS we ar taught in thir words, *In vaine do they worschip me, teaching the doctrines the precepts of men.*

I

The Christian life is an ordered life. We have seen that it has its *basis* in the fact that true knowledge of God is itself, as such, service of God. We have seen that it has its *power* in the fact that Jesus Christ through faith becomes the crisis of our human exist-ence. And we have seen that it has its *essence* in daily repentance, rooted in thankfulness, as man's return to God, who makes amends for the evil we do. By this it is settled that the Christian life is a life deter-mined and regulated by its basis, its power and its essence, and cannot be a life at the mercy of chance or individual will. Do we satisfy the demands of the Christian life thus defined ? Do we do justice to this ordinance which governs it ? We are to deal with that in the following lecture. But whatever our answer may be, it is certain that the Christian life is a life subject to the claims of an ordinance, a life in which obedience of a quite specific character is required of man. Service of God means that our life receives an orientation. Faith means that one thing is enjoined us and another forbidden us. Thankfulness means that we wish to seek the one and shun the other.

Again, the basis, the power and the essence of the Christian life settle another matter too—namely that the ordinance which governs the Christian life cannot be our private concern. When the Scottish Confession speaks of the Law of " good works " it, like the Reformed churches of the sixteenth century in general, has in view two forms of ostensible service of God, both of which fail to understand the fact that the Law and consequently the ordinance governing the Christian life is the *divine* Law. On the one side we have the Roman church which, on the basis of natural rights and its own tradition, both of which it alleges to be divine, dares to subject Christian life to a statute devised and formulated by man and consisting in regulations dealing with cult, law and morals. And on the other side—the opposite extreme—are the varying courses taken by a religious enthusiasm, which wishes to submit Christian life to the dictation of what is called the Spirit, or of an " inner light " which is alleged to be divine, or simply to the dictates of the conscience of every individual. Both these extremes are based on the erroneous belief that the ordinance governing the Christian life is committed

into man's hands. For it obviously amounts to the
same thing whether the place of the Divine Lawgiver
is usurped by a church which decides with divine
authority, or by an individual who decides with divine
freedom. In the one case as in the other we have to
do with a form of false service of God. In both forms
man is secretly his own master; in both forms the
apparent order of the Christian life is really disorder
and in both forms the Christian life is in fact at the
mercy of chance and individual will. When viewed
from the standpoint of the basis, the power and the
essence of the Christian life, and from the standpoint
of the true service of God, neither form can be sub-
stantiated or justified.

The true ordinance governing the Christian life is
Jesus Christ, and it is therefore superior to both the
church and the individual in the church. The authority and freedom which are valid in the Christian
life are the authority and freedom by which Jesus
Christ makes His Word heard and obeyed among
men—and His Word means Himself. It is He who
says what is good or evil, enjoined or forbidden. It
is He and He alone who is also the judge, before
whom we have to justify ourselves. Article 14 speaks
of the Ten Commandments. Now the Ten Commandments are the Divine Law of the Christian life,
because in their two parts—not to be separated nor
confused—in the Commandments of the two Tables,
they bear witness to Jesus Christ as our Lord, by
claiming us for *God* and our *fellow-men*. " Both
[tables] " as the Scottish Confession says, " have the
reveiled will of God for their assurance." Therefore

their authority does not rest on natural rights, nor on church tradition, nor on the voice of the individual conscience either, but on the revealed will of God. And the revealed will of God is Jesus Christ. In Him (according to Ephesians 2, 10, quoted at the beginning of Article 13)—in Him " we are created unto good works, which God hath before ordained, that we should walk in them."

II

The Divine Law regulates the Christian life in the relationship of man to *God*. The Divine Law *enjoins* us to give God the glory, to call on Him as helper in every time of need, to fear His name, to hear and obey His Word, to make use of the means of His grace. And the Divine Law *forbids* us to seek help from other powers, to despise His Word, to worship idols, to take His name in vain, to falsify in any way or still worse to ignore the means of His grace. Such, according to the Scottish Confession, is the first table, the ordinance governing the Christian life in its relation to God. The thankfulness of faith inevitably and invariably takes the form that we in our relation to God do certain things and leave others undone, not because we believe some to be good and others to be evil, but because some are enjoined us and others forbidden by the revealed will of God. But what we have to understand and explain at this point is *how far* this command and prohibition is the revealed will of God and therefore the ordinance from which we cannot escape. To understand and explain this we must go back to that knowledge of God which

comprises and determines true service of God, and
we must return in particular to the knowledge of the
renewing of our nature which has been fully accomplished in Jesus Christ, as is presented in Articles
7-10 of the Confession (Numbers 7 and 8 of our
lectures). We saw there that this renewing of man
and consequently the Christian life consists in Jesus
Christ, as true God, having taken our place. Our
election and salvation, our whole existence, preserved
from judgement and on its way towards eternal life,
rests entirely on the perfection of the eternal God,
who has made Himself in Jesus Christ our Representative, Counsel and Advocate. If we *stand firm*, we do
so by means of God's decision which has already taken
place, and by means of God's work which has already
taken place in Jesus Christ and is real to-day and for
ever. We could only *fall headlong* into the bottomless
pit, if this decision had not been made and this work
not taken place, if it had not been God Himself who
had decided here, and acted, and if Jesus had not been
God's own eternal Son. We are sustained by God's
grace because it is the grace of *God* and not some kindly
piece of help, enlightenment or alleviation, such as
one creature can receive from another, but the omnipotent and perfect support of Him who alone is great
enough to support us effectively in the plight of our
existence. Were God not for us, everything could
not but be against us. But Jesus Christ has come as
true God to us and has taken our place. This is the
reason why we—and with us the Christian life—are
bound with so strong a bond to God in accordance with
the commandments of the first table. In and with

the Gospel of God's great faithfulness and grace there is laid on us the command which bids us do everything which can glorify God as God, and which forbids us to do anything which would rob God of His glory as God. We are God's in Jesus Christ. *That* involves one thing being commanded us and another forbidden. Thus the law of God does not require us to do something which we might equally well leave undone or to leave undone something which we might equally well do. It requires from us nothing more nor less than that we should be what we are, namely, men elected and saved by God in Jesus Christ —and correspondingly that we should not be what we are not, namely, men lost without God and forsaken by Him. Nothing would therefore be further from the truth than, to desire to see in the commands and prohibitions of the first table a demand for a particular form of piety and for certain exceptional religious activities. To serve God by giving Him the glory according to the direction of these commands and prohibitions means not to do something special but to remain in a place where we can breathe and not to enter a place where we would inevitably be suffocated, to be what we are and not to be what we are not. To obey means to assent to the truth and in the truth to assent to our salvation. Not to obey would mean to lie and therefore to assent to our destruction. But we may exist in the truth and so assent to our salvation. For this reason we may and must obey and for this reason our reverence towards God is not something special but the natural expression of the freedom He has given us of being His children.

III

We come now to the Commandments of the second table. The divine law regulates the Christian life in the sphere of man's relation to his *fellow man*. It *enjoins* respect, love and readiness to help in our relations to father and mother and all superiors. It enjoins obedience to them so far as that would not be contrary to obedience to God. It enjoins defiance to tyrants, defence of the weak, chastity and temperance, and an attitude of fairness and consideration to all. And the divine law *forbids* rebellion against lawful authority, murder and what leads to murder and hence even the persisting in wrath, and it forbids looking on inactively where innocent blood is being shed. So runs the second table in the exposition given by the Scottish Confession. We see with particular clearness at this point the decidedly masculine, not to say warlike, spirit of the document. When we come to discuss Article 24, in our last lecture but one, we will have to return to the particularly impressive and original statements it makes here in connection with the sixth commandment. It is no accident that just at this point the Confession reminds us with peculiar clearness of the fact that it was made not by angels but by men in this world in the midst of the rather turbulent Scotland of the sixteenth century. But it is just to the things of this world that the Confession has something to say at this point and not only at this point. What is dealt with here is the ordinance governing the Christian life in its relation to our neighbour. The thankfulness of faith

—and let us note that at this very point disobedience is described as unthankfulness—necessarily and invariably takes this further form of doing one thing and forbearing another in relation to our fellow men as well as to God. Once again we do so not because we hold the one to be good and the other evil and so act out of a sense of humanity, but because the one is enjoined us and the other forbidden us by the revealed will of God.

But here too understanding and explanation are called for. To what extent and for what reason is this command and prohibition the revealed will of God and consequently the ordinance from which we cannot escape? And here also we must go back to that knowledge of God which precedes all true service of God, back to the knowledge of our renewing in Jesus Christ, and hence we must turn back to Articles 7-10 of the Confession. It should be clearly noted that here, in the Christology of the Scottish Confession, we find the source without which it is impossible to understand, let alone to adopt, its doctrine of the divine commandment. We saw in our seventh and eighth lectures that our renewing consists in Jesus Christ as true man taking precisely our place. Our election and salvation and so once again our whole existence is absolutely dependent on the fact that the Son of God came down to us, and became like us and became therefore *a man :* a poor, weak, mortal and dying man, such as we. At the very place where we would have had to stand, God stands as the bearer of the burden which we could not bear, in order that His glory might remain for us. We owe it to His human nature that there is election for *man* on the basis of God's decision and that there is salvation for *man* through the action of God. " For ye know the grace of our Lord Jesus Christ, that, though He was rich, yet for your sakes He became poor, that ye through His poverty might be rich " (2 Cor. 8, 9). If God had not given up His Son for us, we would be and would continue to be most miserable creatures. But because Jesus Christ has come to us as true man and hence has really taken our place, we are bound to our neighbour also. In and with the Gospel of God's condescension to man, the commandment is laid upon us which enjoins us to do all things for our neighbour and nothing against him. We are God's in Jesus Christ. We are therefore and thereby bound to our neighbour. Hence once again it is not true that God's law demands that we do something which we could leave undone or that we leave undone something which we could just as well do. It demands from us neither more nor less than ourselves, as those who have been elected and saved in the poor man Jesus. It demands only that we should be in truth men thus elected and saved. If we are such, then we cannot but recognise in the poor men with whom we have to live—and they really are poor men—the brothers of Jesus, whose presence reminds us all the more of Him, the greater their weakness. They therefore, in their need as men, have a message to bring us from Him for which we owe them thanks and are therefore under an obligation to them. Our relation to them is the sign and the test of our relation to God. " He that loveth not his brother whom he hath seen, how can he love God whom he hath not seen?" (1 John 4, 20). The God whom we do not see has become in Jesus Christ a man whom we do see. We have thereby come to owe every man honour, service and help. Once again the commands and prohibitions of the second table are not to be understood any more than those of the first as the demand for a particular morality or for exceptional achievements of some kind or another in relation to our fellow men. Christianity is not morality. We are not intended to be benefactors or instructors, much less gods to one another. We are not doing anything special when we love one another. In doing this we are simply doing the one thing most natural for those chosen and saved in Jesus Christ, we are simply doing the one thing necessary, which we as brothers owe one another, because we owe it to Jesus Christ. In doing this we are simply being obedient. And once again our obedience will be not something special but only the natural expression of the freedom which is bestowed upon us by God Himself becoming our brother in Jesus Christ.

IV

The subject of our enquiry has been the ordinance of the Christian life, the true way of thankfulness and of repentance and the criterion of good and evil. The Ten Commandments which we have expounded are the testimony to this ordinance, this way and this criterion. They are this in so far as they, as the ordinance governing the life of the people of God, bear witness to the Lord of this people and hence to our Lord and to His will with us. Jesus Christ, by making us free, binds us to God and man. As God's Son He binds us to God, and as Mary's son, born in the manger and crucified on the Cross, He binds us to man. This is the claim, twofold but indivisible, which is laid upon us. The Law, the rule and the first principles underlying all service of God are— *Jesus Christ.* And we say nothing other than this, when we say *faith* in Jesus Christ. For by faith in Him it is true for us and it becomes true for our life, that Jesus Christ as true God and true man stands in our place. By faith He dwells in our hearts and rules our thoughts, words and deeds. Our faith is certainly weak and small. But Jesus Christ, who by faith dwells in our hearts, is strong and great. And because of this, however weak and small our faith may be, it is none the less true to say, that by faith is bestowed upon us the ordinance of the Christian life, the way of thankfulness and repentance and the criterion of good and evil, and further that faith will never be without love and hence without the fulfilling of the divine law, and finally that all our works which proceed from faith will be good works.

THE TRUE CHRISTIAN LIFE

(Art. 15)

ART. XV

OF THE PERFECTIOUN OF THE LAW, AND THE IMPERFECTIOUN OF MAN

The 'Law of God we confesse and acknawledge maist just, maist equall, maist halie, and maist perfite, commaunding thir thingis, quhilk being wrocht in perfectioun, were abill to give life, and abill to bring man to eternall felicitie. Bot our nature is sa corrupt, sa weake, and sa unperfite, that we ar never abill to fulfill the warkes of the Law in perfectioun. Zea, gif we say we have na sinne, evin after we ar regenerate, we deceive our selves, and the veritie of God is not in us. And therefore, it behovis us to apprehend *Christ Jesus* with his justice and satisfaction, quha is the end and accomplishment of the Law, be quhome we ar set at this liberty, that the curse and male-diction of God fall not upon us, albeit we fulfill not the same in al pointes. For God the Father beholding us, in the body of his Sonne *Christ Jesus*, acceptis our imperfite obedience, as it were perfite, and covers our warks, quhilk ar defyled with mony spots, with the justice of his Sonne. We do not meane that we ar so set at liberty, that we awe na obedience to the Law (for that before wee have plainly confessed), bot this we affirme, that na man in eird (*Christ Jesus* onlie except) hes given, gives, or sall give in worke, that obedience to the Law, quhilk the Law requiris. Bot when we have done all things, we must falle down and unfeinedly confesse, that we are unprofitable servands. And therefore, quhosoever boastis themselves of the merits of their awin works, or put their trust in the works of Supererogation, boast themselves in that quhilk is nocht, and put their trust in damnable Idolatry.

I

We have spoken in the last lecture but one of the *real* Christian life. It consists in daily thankfulness and repentance, as the reiteration of faith in Jesus Christ, which is the work of the Holy Spirit. And we have spoken in our last lecture of the *Ordinance* governing the Christian life. It, too, consists in faith in Jesus Christ, in so far as such faith leads us of necessity to love for God and man. Our enquiry is now directed to the *true* Christian life. The heading of Article 15 of the Scottish Confession makes very clear what the problem is, which is raised and has to be answered here. It runs " Of the perfectioun of the Law and the imperfectioun of man," or as the Latin version of the Confession puts it, " The Law is perfect in every respect, but men are imperfect." What does this imply ? Once this is established it raises the question of the true Christian life. " True " according to the usage of Scripture is that which is real and which corresponds to the claim contained in its concept, that is, what is based on itself and authentic. Is there a true Christian life ? Is there genuine and authentic thankfulness and repentance ? Is there a fulfilling of the Law ? Is it a fact that there are men who obey God ? If the Law is perfect, while man is imperfect, then this question has to be faced. We have to bear in mind that we are not dealing with any kind of law or other, capable of imperfect as well as perfect fulfilment. We all consider ourselves acquainted with a moral law of some sort or other, and know that our fulfilment of it is never more than approximate and therefore imperfect. But the very approximation, which we believe we have attained, does none the less console us for our imperfection. In spite of this imperfection we would scarcely allow ourselves to be persuaded that our moral life was for that reason unreal and unreliable. We do strive for perfection—who would not ?—we all do it—and our true moral life consists in that very fact. But the true Christian life cannot so easily be rendered compatible with our imperfection, even though we were to strive to attain the perfection of its ordinance. The reason for this is that the ordinance governing the Christian life is the Divine Law. But this law makes an unconditional demand upon us. What is our position then ? Either we are thankful or we are not. Either we are penitent or we are not. Either we love God and our neighbour or we hate them both. Either we are obedient or we are not. There is no possibility here of a third, middle course, consisting in some sort of approximation, in which we might find our consolation. In this fact consists the perfection of the Divine Law. Question 62 of the Heidelberg Catechism on this point reads " The righteousness which can stand before the judgement seat of God must be perfect throughout and wholly conformable to the Divine Law." Imperfection here means disobedience and thus unrighteousness. But man is imperfect. That statement, if meant in a moral sense, is a commonplace that has never cost any of us a single moment's sleep. It does not trouble us. We can put up with it. But if meant in a Christian sense, it is a judgement which would inevitably destroy us, because it calls in question and indeed denies that our Christian life is true and thereby denies our salvation. God's Law enjoins thankfulness, penitence and love to God and one's neighbour. Man with all his outward and inward achievements, with his thoughts and feelings as well as his deeds, stands in the presence of that Law as one who is unthankful and impenitent, and who, since he does not love God or his neighbour, must hate them ; or who is there who could stand at any time before God's Law in any other guise ? Whoever would make such a claim, could only have some other law in mind, and not the Divine Law. Thus man stands there as a transgressor of the Law, and his life, considered as a Christian life, is not genuine or reliable, and therefore not true. Thus it is not a Christian life at all.

What is the true Christian life, which, since it can only be discerned from its ordinance, from the Divine Law governing the Christian life, cannot at any rate be discovered in our life as such, in our outward and inward achievements, but is in fact called in question, or indeed denied in this life of ours ?

The Scottish Confession is put to the test and we with it, if an answer is to be given to this. On this question as to the true Christian life a decision has to be made. We are so to speak on a razor's edge. What is our life ? Is Jesus Christ our Life ? This should clearly be so, if the Christian life is the point at issue and the subject of the enquiry. But when we do not think, or do not think seriously, that it is the Christian life, about which enquiry is being made, and that Jesus Christ is our life, when this is to us

merely a pious phrase, good enough for hymns and
edifying addresses and prayers, but of no practical
importance as an answer to the question about our
true life—when we really are seeking and finding
our life in ourselves, in the attitudes we take up, in
sentiments which we make our own and in actions
which we can perform—what then? We are faced
with a dilemma. Either we recognise that there is no
Christian life for us, and so no life of obedience to
God, thereby signing our death warrants, so that we
may thereafter give ourselves over to frivolity and
despair, or—what is still worse—we bury our heads
in the sand like an ostrich, i.e. we persuade ourselves
that the law to which we are subject is in no sense the
perfect and majestic Law of God, but simply the moral
law, which we feel ourselves quite able to satisfy to a
certain extent. And under its rule we have rest, or
at least we can forget that the life we live without
peace with God is a lost one.

The Scottish Confession pre-supposes that *Jesus
Christ* is our life, and we also, in accordance with all
we have so far learnt from it, will likewise have to
pre-suppose this—and do so in no rhetorical sense
but in all seriousness and in reality. This is the same
as to say *faith* in Jesus Christ is our life. We live
precisely in so far as we believe, and allow God in
Jesus Christ to be our Lord. And that once more is
the same as to say that we live precisely in so far as
God lives in Jesus Christ and is our Lord and permits
and commands us to live in Him. Not before Him
or behind Him, below Him or above Him or beside
Him, but *in* Him. For to be before Him, behind,

below, above or beside Him is not life, because it is not reconciliation or fellowship between God and man. But these are in Him and therefore in Him is our life. He Himself *is* our life. If that holds good, then the question regarding the true Christian life appears in a different light. In that case it is not imperfect and thus disobedient man, who faces the perfect Law of God, which is the inviolable ordinance of this life. Our life as our own, whether we admit it or not, would only come under the power of the judgement, which would ultimately destroy it. But where we with our life, as our own, would have had to stand, there Jesus Christ stands, and He is our life. Thus the question about our true life is also directed to Him. And this, according to the Scottish Confession, is the real question about the true *Christian* life. For this reason the answer also will turn out to be different from what it would have been, had we stood before the Divine Law with our life as our own, with our sentiments and actions, and had to justify ourselves before that law. We saw in the previous lecture that Jesus Christ Himself, as true God and true man is the Divine *Law* to which we are subject. We must now go further. He, as true God and true man, is also the *fulfilment* of the Law. Where is thankfulness to be found, or penitence, or love to God and man in accordance with the requirements of the Ten Commandments? In our life as our own we shall look in vain for true obedience to these requirements. But we shall not look in vain to Jesus Christ, His suffering and obedience, for the fulfilment of the Law and the doing of the will of God. And now His life is our life. Now He has done what He has done, in our place and for our sake. So now we have done —in Him—what He has done, and so the Divine acknowledgement of His obedience benefits us directly. In Him the Christian life is true—and in Him alone —but in Him as our own Christian life, our thankfulness is true and our penitence, our love to God and man is true, and our service of God is true. It is true, because, and so far as, it is faith in Jesus Christ.

II

The enquiry into the true Christian life finds its answer, once we believe that it is answered in Jesus Christ. But the question is capable of rising again and returning in a foolish form. The Scottish Confession has rightly considered it necessary to answer the question as put in this foolish form also. Does not our Christian life, the question runs, always remain our own life as such and apart from faith, apart from Jesus Christ? We have heard of the conflict in which it really is engaged. Are we not perhaps, since we are certain of our true Christian life in Jesus Christ, discharged from this conflict and from our duty of obedience? Once our relation to God has been set in order by faith in Jesus Christ, does there not perhaps exist apart from faith a sphere of life, or even many such spheres in which our action is subject to chance, or indeed to the moral law or to other laws as well (perhaps to those of biology, æsthetics, economics or politics)? These would be spheres of life in which we, while recognising and acknowledging the

142

imperfection of this world, could yet remain satisfied with our honest endeavour after perfection of many kinds. Is the truth that our true Christian life is our life in Jesus Christ not after all a particular, a " religious " truth, which certainly assures us of Heaven, but alongside of which there exists a whole universe of truth about life from a quite different source ? Does our life in Jesus Christ not immediately exempt us from the necessity of being subject to the Divine Law in our own life also, as it is enacted in this world, in the form of our personal ways of thought and action ? To this foolish question the Scottish Confession gives the prompt and clear answer that all that is quite out of the question ; Jesus Christ, He and He alone, is the true Christian life, and that does not mean the beginning of a *new* emancipation, but the end of *all* emancipation. It does not mean that we are exempted from the Law, but that we are now for the first time really and completely subjected to it, precisely by the fact that we recognise its fulfilment in Jesus Christ and in Him alone. Our life as such, our human life in its total extent, our ways of thought and of action, our outward and inward achievements, could not have a more intensive and complete claim made upon them than is made by our believing in Jesus Christ and by His being thus our life. How could all this be anything other than a circle which, whether it be narrow or wide, has this and this only as its centre ? How could chance or morality or any other arbitrary factor set up its own special law here ? How could it be possible for us to rest satisfied with our own imperfections ? How could there be

room there for any other truth about life ? Because
Jesus Christ in His obedience and suffering takes our
place, in order to make amends for the evil that we do,
we with our whole life, as ours, become and remain
bound to Him as to the Divine Law. It is not a
matter of our fulfilling the Law with this life of ours:
But it is equally not a matter of this life of ours being
withdrawn from the Law or of our being permitted
at any part of it, under any condition or at any time,
to have any other desire than to show gratitude and
penitence and to love God and our neighbour. Our
true action is the action of Jesus Christ, but it is required of us as our action. What if we should object
that as our action it will always be insincere, superficial
and imperfect ? The answer to that would be that
all criticism of this nature, whether justified or un-
justified, is far out-distanced by the acknowledgement
which our obedience, as faith in Jesus Christ, has
already found with God, whatever the nature of this
obedience may be. It is just through this acknowledgement that we are translated into the realm of obedience
and sustained in it, be the nature of this obedience
what it may, regardless of the results of our self-
criticism. As Martin Niemoeller wrote in a letter
from prison, " We have not to ask how far we are to
rely upon ourselves, but we are asked whether we
rely on God's Word as being God's Word, and as
doing what it says." By relying on God's Word
as being God's Word and doing what it says, we are
and continue to be summoned, set in motion, impelled
to gratitude and repentance and to love for God and
man, under all conditions and without intermission.

144

Provision for our sanctification here in time is made by our justification before God having taken place once and for all in Jesus Christ, and by our having the right to believe in it.

III

The question as to the true Christian life is answered, once we believe that its answer lies in Jesus Christ. But it is capable of rising again and returning in yet another foolish form. The Scottish Confession has rightly provided an explicit answer to this formulation of the question as well. Is not our life, the question runs, when lived in faith and as in Jesus Christ none the less our own ? Is it not formed by our ways of thought and action and by definite thoughts, words and works which are our own and which are good in themselves ? Could it not then, to some extent, become and be in and of itself a true Christian life, obedience and fulfilment of the Law, and so be in a certain sense independent of Jesus Christ ? Could there not exist a Christian sphere in human life, it may be that of Christian worship or even that of an entire Christian culture, or at least that of specifically Christian customs and morality, in which man, though certainly not without the Grace of God, could yet in a real sense deserve well of God and of God's cause on earth ? Might not man, therefore, have the right to look upon such a sphere of life with the confidence of having done his duty and perhaps even more than his duty here, and therefore with the confidence of standing before God justified and commended not only in Jesus Christ but also in this work of his own and to this extent in himself? This position, too, is promptly and clearly rejected by the Scottish Confession. A Christianity which is separate and independent, i.e. distinct from the righteousness of Christ, it calls idoiatry. The Confession cites the saying of Jesus " When ye shall have done all those things which are commanded you, say, we are unprofitable servants " (Luke 17, 10). In those days it was against Roman Catholicism that this answer was directed. But we must not overlook the fact that to-day it can be applied to a great extent to the theory and practice of the Evangelical churches as well.* But after all that has been said, there can be no doubt that we too must adopt this answer of the Confession for ourselves. The fact is that Jesus Christ and He alone is and remains the true Christian life. Through Him we are summoned to obedience and set in motion, and that does not mean the beginning of a *new* self-righteousness but the end of *all* self-righteousness. It does not mean that we are invited to have a new confidence in ourselves, but to put our entire confidence in Jesus Christ alone. It is solely in this confidence in Him that we shall be able to render the obedience required of us. By trusting in ourselves we could only become disobedient. It is just when we are obedient and when, according to God's true judgement, we have done " those things which are commanded us," that we shall hold fast to this one fact, that this judgement of God is grace and therefore

* The Confession is opposed, and rightly so, to all talk about the goodness of the Christian life.

unmerited judgement, not based on our fulfilling of the Law nor on the sincerity, depth and perfection of our outward and inward achievements, nor on any particular " Christian character " in them. We may be right or wrong about such self-esteem. But it is out-distanced, just as we saw was the case with our self-criticism. It is outdistanced by the imperfection and hence the unrighteousness in which we stand before God, as soon as we consider ourselves apart from Jesus Christ, even when our works are our best, our hearts at their noblest and our achievements most brilliant. If we wish to see our righteousness before God, our true Christian life, its true glory and its true merits, then we must not consider ourselves apart from Jesus Christ but in Him and in Him alone. If we wish to know a foundation on which we can stand and stand firmly with confidence, we must know that our sins are forgiven us in Him. We place no confidence then, not even a secondary, supplementary confidence, in the worth and value of what we have achieved in the human sphere. The more serious and the greater this achievement is, and it may be great and serious, the more shall we " set our hopes in grace alone " (1 Peter 1, 13), and we shall not doubt, but hope just as certainly that that achievement could not be greater or more serious, nor the true Christian life shine brighter than where the grace of Our Lord Jesus Christ is acknowledged without reserve as the first and last word about the true Christian life.

THE MYSTERY OF THE CHURCH

(Art. 16-17, 25*a*)

ART. XVI

OF THE KIRK

As we beleve in ane God, Father, Sonne, and haly Ghaist ; sa do
we maist constantly beleeve, that from the beginning there hes
bene, and now is, and to the end of the warld sall be, ane Kirk,
that is to say, ane company and multitude of men chosen of
God, who richtly worship and imbrace him be trew faith in
Christ Jesus, quha is the only head of the same Kirk, quhilk
alswa is the bodie and spouse of *Christ Jesus*, quhilk Kirk is
catholike, that is, universal, because it conteinis the Elect of
all ages, of all realmes, nations, and tongues, be they of the
Jewes, or be they of the Gentiles, quha have communion and
societie with God the Father, and with his Son *Christ Jesus*,
throw the sanctificatioun of his haly Spirit : and therefore it
is called the communioun, not of prophane persounes, bot of
Saincts, quha as citizenis of the heavenly *Jerusalem*, have the
fruitioun of the maist inestimable . benefites, to wit, of ane
God, ane Lord *Jesus*, ane faith, and ane baptisme : Out of the
quhilk Kirk, there is nouther lyfe, nor eternall felicitie.   And
therefore we utterly abhorre the blasphemie of them that
affirme, that men quhilk live according to equitie and justice,
sal be saved, quhat Religioun that ever they have professed.
For as without *Christ Jesus* there is nouther life nor salvation ;
so sal there nane be participant therof, bot sik as the Father
hes given unto his Sonne *Christ Jesus*, and they that in time
cum unto him, avowe his doctrine, and beleeve into him, we
comprehend the children with the faithfull parentes.   This
Kirk is invisible, knawen onelie to God, quha alane knawis
whome he hes chosen ; and comprehends as weill (as said

is) the Elect that be departed, commonlie called the *Kirk Triumphant*, and they that zit live and fecht against sinne and *Sathan* as sall live hereafter.

ART. XVII

OF THE IMMORTALITIE OF THE SAULES

The Elect departed are in peace and rest fra their labours : Not that they sleep, and come to a certaine oblivion, as some Phantastickes do affirme ; bot that they are delivered fra all feare and torment, and all temptatioun, to quhilk we and all Goddis Elect are subject in this life, and therefore do beare the name of the *Kirk Militant :* As contrariwise, the reprobate and unfaithfull departed have anguish, torment, and paine, that cannot be expressed. Sa that nouther are the ane nor the uther in sik sleepe that they feele not joy or torment, as the Parable of *Christ Jesus* in the 16th of *Luke*, his words to the thiefe, and thir wordes of the saules crying under the Altar, *O Lord, thou that art righteous and just, How lang sall thou not revenge our blude upon thir that dwellis in the Eird ?* dois testifie.

ART. XXV

OF THE GUIFTES FREELY GIVEN TO THE KIRK

Albeit that the Worde of God trewly preached, and the Sacraments richtlie ministred, and Discipline executed according to the Worde of God, be the certaine and infallible Signes of the trew Kirk, we meane not that everie particular persoun joyned with sik company, be ane elect member of *Christ Jesus :* For we acknawledge and confesse, that Dornell, Cockell, and Caffe may be sawen, grow, and in great aboundance lie in the middis of the Wheit, that is, the Reprobate may be joyned in the societie of the Elect, and may externally use with them the benefites of the worde and Sacraments : Bot sik being bot temporall professoures in mouth, but not in heart, do fall backe, and continew not to the end. And therefore have they na fruite of *Christs* death, Resurrection nor Ascension.

I

There exists what we may call a *vertical* view of true service of God or the true Christian life. When we understand the Christian life in the light of its origin and object, it is simply and without reservation the life of Jesus Christ Himself, so far as men through God's Holy Spirit are united with Him in faith, so far as His life becomes theirs and their life His. It is of this vertical view of the Christian life that we have been speaking till now. We have seen in our last lecture that the determination of the Christian life by Jesus Christ is a total one; beyond and beside it there exists neither a general nor a special true Christian life. This total claim is the last word in the matter. The other or what we may call the *horizontal* view of the same reality will not cancel or even limit this totality; it can only confirm it. And there does exist such a second horizontal view of this reality, confirming and reiterating the first view. We are not introducing it arbitrarily. On the contrary, this reality itself requires this second view of it. If the Christian life is the life of Jesus Christ, then that implies that the life of this one person is the life of *many*, the life of a *people*. If their true life only exists in this One and in faith in Him, yet this One does not live His own life for Himself and for His own sake. On the contrary, having life in Himself, He pours it forth on those who through the Holy Spirit have their life in Him by faith. They it is who are united and formed into this people. They it is who by virtue of their common descent, history and speech together form the area within which Jesus Christ lives His divine life in human form, that is as the Reconciler of men and as the true Christian life upon earth. They it is in whose midst the sign and the signs of the Divine election and calling of man have been set up and are being set up again and again. The " many," this people, this area and these signs in the midst of this area have been referred to by the Scottish Confession from the very beginning—we recall our sixth lecture on article 5. We saw then that this people of Jesus Christ's is the people of Israel ; in it, in its area, under the sign given it are gathered together the many who are reconciled with God in Jesus Christ and who, being thus reconciled, have a right to proclaim His glory, as they serve Him in gratitude and repentance. The people of Israel was never identical with the Jewish people, as a natural entity. On the contrary, if the Jewish people has received and to this day never lost the promise that it is the people to whom God will reveal His Glory, none the less this promise is one to which it has never had either a natural or an exclusive claim. That became manifest when it rejected its Messiah and delivered Him up to the judgement and power of Pilate, a Gentile judge. With this rejecting and delivering up of the Messiah by the Jews, and with what the Gentiles then did to Him, the door, which had never been closed, was thrown wide open. His people, that disobedient people among whom and for whom He suffered, is the Israel which is gathered together by the Holy Spirit, the Israel of *all* those who have become debtors to Him, and who have been freed by Him, the *one Holy* Church of Jews *and* Gentiles. Despite the differences in earthly descent, this people is *united* by its common origin in the Crucified Son of God. Despite the differences in the temporal and historical situation of its members, it is united by their common experience under the guidance and in the keeping of the one Lord. Despite the differences in natural languages, it is united by the common language of the Holy Spirit, who speaks of the great acts of God. Despite the differences between the living and the dead, it is united by the common benefit which we may yet receive, while those who are dead have already received it once and for all—as is worked out in Article 17 of the Confession. And this people is *sanctified* despite the fact that it is a disobedient people, as is unmistakeably clear in the light of its origin in the Cross of Christ. It is sanctified through Him who makes the ungodly righteous, through the election and calling of its Lord and Head, through its being free in faith to assent to its salvation. Such is the horizontal view of the Christian life. Such is the life of the *Church* of Jesus Christ ; that it is one and is holy is certainly hidden and is a matter for faith. But that it exists is manifest and can be seen as well as believed. As a divine establishment and foundation it is hidden, but as a human assembly and community it is manifest. As the Israel which is born of the Word and the Spirit and the people to whom God will reveal His glory it is hidden, but it is manifest as the historical form of Christendom. As the body and bride of Jesus Christ it is hidden, but it is manifest wherever men " richtly worship and imbrace [God] be trew faith in *Christ Jesus*," as the Scottish Confession says. I repeat, with a slight alteration, " it is manifest wherever men wish truly and obediently to worship God and to embrace Him through faith in Jesus Christ."

II

Real service of God, the true Christian life on the one hand, and on the other the life of the one holy church, these two are distinguishable in thought, but not in reality. Where there was no Christian life there would be no church. But also where there was no church, there would be no Christian life. " Out of the quhilk Kirk, there is nouther lyfe, nor eternall felicitie," as the Confession says. For Jesus Christ, Whose life is the Christian life, does live in God, and does sit at the right hand of the Father in His everlasting kingdom and hence in measureless exaltation over His church, as her Heavenly and Invisible Head. But there also He is the One, who as God humbled Himself in order that as man He might be exalted. Hence in Heaven, too, He is our Mediator, Advocate and High Priest. Hence there, too, He is not without His people, the many elected and called by Him, who are one with Him through faith here on earth and in time. And so conversely He lives for us on earth and in time nowhere else than in the midst of his people, as the meaning and content of *its* history, the ground and truth of the promise made to *it* and the object of *its* faith. Jesus Christ lives by the tidings about Him being proclaimed and heard. This is His life on earth.

153

He lives where two or three are gathered together in His name. He lives where men hope to be united to Him and so to be sanctified by Him as a body. He lives as king by the actualisation of His lordship. All this means that He lives in His church. It is true that He lives in His church, as it is hidden and not as it is manifest. But He lives in His church and not outside it, i.e. not in such a way that one could seek Him and shun His people, or love Him and hate His people. And neither is there any faith, active in love, possessed by an individual, such that the individual could regard and treat it as his own private concern. This is the great error, which since the seventeenth century has prevailed in modern Protestantism. Religion is perhaps a private matter. But we are speaking here not of religion but of faith, and that cannot be a private matter. In the Christian life we are not concerned with our becoming Christian personalities or with such personalities, being like minded, subsequently becoming united in one way or another. All that—Christian personalities and the union of them—can be very fine, but yet it looks as if there were already in process here another instance of the idolatry in which man wishes really to make his own achievements the basis of his confidence. The one and only thing with which we are concerned in the Christian life is our becoming members of the Israel which is born of the Word and the Spirit. Real service of God takes place in the fellowship of the one holy church or it does not take place at all. Real service of God does consist in our believing in Jesus Christ and in accepting the fact that He lives

His life in our stead and for our sake. But His life as the life of the Head is not to be separated from the life of the body, nor His life as the life of the One from the life of the many. If His life is our life, then our life must be the life of members of His body. We, too, cannot remain without, but because He is within His church, we must likewise be within and with Him. We must guard against very easy but false analogies. One can be a good citizen without belonging to a political party. One can be musical without joining a choral society. One can be a philosopher and as an eclectic or sceptic stand aloof from all philosophical movements, and the great philosophers are always above these. But one cannot hold the Christian faith without holding it in the church and with the church. The church is neither a party nor a society nor a movement. She is the form in which the Christian faith exists, because it is faith in the One who died and rose again for the many. Such a content *must* have and can *only* have this form.

III

We have already said that the Christian life or the life of the church is not only invisible, but is also visible and public. It is, as we have seen, visible and public wherever men rightly and obediently worship God, and through true faith in Jesus Christ wish to embrace Him. It is visible wherever men confess this faith that is in them and wish to submit themselves and their actions to God's commandments. How could it be other than visible and public? There is no lack of those who wish in an equally visible and public way not to do this. The church possesses an appearance and a form by which she is distinguished from other forms and through which her existence can immediately be established by any man. This appearance, which she possesses, has features which are fair and elevating and others which are ugly and disappointing. It depends on the point of view from which you consider the church, whether you see and stress the one or the other more. Both points of view are true. On the one side are her treasures, which have grown greater and greater in the course of her long history, human greatness, heroism, profound thought, love, epoch-making achievements, and quiet but not unsuccessful educational work among the nations and among countless individuals. This is the one side. But on the other side *—everything human has always another side too—there is a slough of human folly and wickedness, senseless conservatism and an even far more senseless mania for modernisation ; the most serious errors even by the greatest men of the church, and that at the place too where the light seems to shine brightest ; fearful disruption and dark stains at the very spot where you might wish to rejoice the most. Such is church history and such too the church in the present age, i.e. in her visible and public form. May one not in the end rejoice despite the evil, or must one not bow one's head and mourn in the end in spite of the good ? Over this optimists and pessimists may dispute. Only both

* Goethe once said that the whole of church history is a jumble of error and force.

sides should not forget that the object of which both are speaking and which both judge according to its visible form, is possessed of a mystery. The true Christian life, the unity and holiness of the church, is nowhere visible or public. It is not something which can immediately be established by anyone. It is in Jesus Christ that she possesses her true nature, unity and holiness—not in what the men gathered together in her, as men, even the greatest and most serious of them, are, say and do, but in what Jesus Christ is for them, has said to them and done for them. She possesses her true nature, unity and holiness in the hidden work of the Holy Spirit, in His electing, calling, directing and comforting. What we see are men, who in all sorts of ways wish to embrace Jesus Christ by faith. But the truth lies not in what men wish, but in what God wills. That is something which in its very nature we do not see, not even where the church seems to show us its brilliant side. God's thoughts are not our thoughts. The optimists in the church ought to be reminded of that. But the same holds true on the negative side, for the pessimists as well. Should the true nature and so the unity and holiness of the church actually disappear and should she have become not the church of Jesus Christ but an empty form deserted by God, that too will not be visible and public, but will be hidden, a judgement passed by God and therefore not to be passed by men. Once again God's thoughts are not our thoughts. If what we see can be no ground for ascribing the presence of the Holy Spirit to the church, neither can it be a ground for denying it. What we see are

men, who want to apprehend Jesus Christ in faith
after a manner that is to us hardly comprehensible
or perhaps not comprehensible at all. But how do
we know that they have not succeeded in doing so
after all, if for all that, Jesus Christ has apprehended
them. "Who art thou that judgest another man's
servant; to his own master he standeth or falleth.
Yea, he shall be holden up; for God is able to make
him stand" (Romans 14, 4), a verse always to be re-
membered. This is what the pessimists must be
told. The true nature, unity and holiness of the
church is the *mystery* of the church. How could it
be anything else, when her life is actually the life of
Jesus Christ Himself?

IV

The road which leads from the outward form of the
church to its mystery, from her two-sided visible and
public character to her true nature, unity and holiness,
is the road of faith. This road cannot be avoided,
but must be taken again and again. If we do not
take it, we are doomed here as elsewhere to sway about
hopelessly, as on a see-saw, between the extremities
of a foolish optimism and a foolish pessimism. In
that case we are members of the church, to-day eager
and enthusiastic and to-morrow tired and sceptical.
Members? No, not members, but spectators, keen
to-day and tired to-morrow, comparable with the
spectators of a game, at one moment clapping and at
another booing, interested perhaps owing to some bet
on the result, but with it all merely showing that they

are not really taking part in the game, but merely looking on. The players themselves have not taken on bets, are not clapping or booing—but are playing. That is what taking part means, and it is just the same in the church—to take part in the life of the church means to have faith. Our faith is what decides that we are members of the church and not mere spectators. And it is precisely faith which decides that we are taking a part not only in the visible, public form of the church, but at the same time in its true nature, unity and holiness. By assenting in faith to Jesus Christ as our Lord, we have already received and given ourselves the answer to the question about the one, true and holy church. We have then sought and found the church in Him as her Head, far beyond all visible human greatness or all visible human misery. Whoever wished to seek for her anywhere else would seek for ever in vain. In this seeking and finding of faith the church lives, whether her form be one in which she is more surrounded by splendour or by misery. But this faith here in time is always a decision. We are not yet in the " ecclesia trumphans " in which, as Article 17 of the Confession says, we shall be " delivered fra all feare and torment and all temptatioun " but we are in the " ecclesia militans," which can only exist from century to century and from day to day through the actualisation of the faith of its living members. For this very reason this seeking and finding of faith cannot mean that we are removed from the human, public life of the church, or can escape from it. How could a man who would withdraw from her temporal form have a share in her

divine, hidden life ? Would that not mean that he
would be withdrawing himself from honest seeking
and finding and would thus be withdrawing himself
from the Lord of the church ? Could he reach the
goal, who did not wish to travel the road to it ? But
the road begins with the human, historical, earthly
form of the church. We are not to come to a stand-
still beside this form, whether as optimists or as pessimists. But we may not leave it behind us either. For
the life of the " ecclesia militans " consists in her
having again and again to *become* a church through
the decision of faith. She is not the church, she
becomes the church again and again. She became
this yesterday. The decisions of faith of those who
went before us have brought us here. And through
the decisions of our faith it will come about to-morrow
too that she will become a church, the one, true and
holy church of Jesus Christ, i.e. the visible form in
which the Lord, as the Mystery of the church, will
come into contact with the many who will come
after us.

THE FORM OF THE CHURCH

(Art. 18*a*)

ART XVIII

OF THE NOTIS, BE THE QUHILK THE TREWE KIRK
IS DECERNIT FRA THE FALSE, AND QUHA SALL BE
JUDGE OF THE DOCTRINE.

Because that *Sathan* from the beginning hes laboured to deck his
pestilent Synagoge with the title of the Kirk of God, and hes
inflamed the hertes of cruell murtherers to persecute, trouble,
and molest the trewe Kirk and members thereof, as *Cain* did
Abell, Ismael Isaac, Esau Jacob, and the haill Priesthead of the
Jewes Christ Jesus himselfe, and his Apostles after him. It
is ane thing maist requisite, that the true Kirk be decerned
fra the filthie Synagogues, be cleare and perfite notes, least
we being deceived, receive and imbrace, to our awin con-
demnatioun, the ane for the uther. The notes, signes, and
assured takens whereby the immaculate Spouse of *Christ Jesus*
is knawen fra the horrible harlot, the Kirk malignant, we
affirme, are nouther Antiquitie, Title usurpit, lineal Descence,
Place appointed, nor multitude of men approving ane error.
For *Cain*, in age and title, was preferred to *Abel* and *Seth :*
Jerusalem had prerogative above all places of the eird, where
alswa were the Priests lineally descended fra *Aaron*, and greater
number followed the Scribes, Pharisies, and Priestes, then
unfainedly beleeved and approved *Christ Jesus* and his doctrine :
And zit, as we suppose, no man of sound judgement will grant,
that ony of the forenamed were the Kirk of God. The notes
therefore of the trew Kirk of God we beleeve, confesse, and
avow to be, first, the trew preaching of the Worde of God,
into the quhilk God hes revealed himselfe unto us, as the

L   161

writings of the Prophets and Apostles dois declair. Secundly, the right administration of the Sacraments of *Christ Jesus*, quhilk man be annexed unto the word and promise of God, to seale and confirme the same in our hearts. Last, Ecclesiastical discipline uprightlie ministred, as Goddis Worde prescribes, whereby vice is repressed, and vertew nurished. Wheresoever then thir former notes are seene, and of ony time continue (be the number never so fewe, about two or three), there, without all doubt, is the trew Kirk of *Christ :* Who, according unto his promise, is in the middis of them. Not that universall, of quhilk we have before spoken, bot particular, sik as wes in *Corinthus*, *Galatia*, *Ephesus*, and uther places, in quhilk the ministrie wes planted be *Paull*, and were of himselfe named the kirks of God.

I

We have seen in our last lecture that the divine mystery of the church is not identical with her human form, but we must seek the divine mystery of the church in her human form ; otherwise we shall never find it. This form is, however, decisively conditioned by the fact that churches are *individual* and therefore *many* in number. The one holy church exists as a form only in such individuality and plurality. Only when sought in these, can she be found. For this reason the New Testament itself speaks of the *Church*, in speaking of the *churches*, and in speaking of the *churches* speaks of course immediately and directly of the *Church* also. The *Church* in the New Testament is the church in Ephesus, the church in Corinth, the church in Rome side by side. Conversely the church in Ephesus, in Corinth and in Rome side by side are in each case the *Church*. What on the other hand is utterly foreign to the New Testament is the conception only too familiar to us of an all inclusive church, whether already organised, or to be organised, or merely as an ideal to which the individual churches would stand in the relation of component churches. And this conception, only too common among us, could hardly be justified from the nature of the thing itself. Jesus Christ is one and does not exist in component parts. And if the church is the form of His earthly human existence during the time between His Ascension and His Second Coming she too cannot exist in parts, but must exist as a whole wherever she exists. She is in that case always the church as a whole in this place and in that, but not the sum of these churches, as though the individual churches were individual numbers, nor is she the harmony of them as if they were individual notes or instruments forming an orchestra. Wherever a church considers herself as a part of the church alongside other parts and is not conscious in all seriousness of being in her individuality the whole church, she has not yet understood herself or taken herself seriously as the church, that is, as an assembly of people under one head Jesus Christ. An association, in view of the idea underlying it and in view of its task, can share with other associations, possessing the same idea and task, in the carrying out of these, so that one association gives more prominence and attention to one side of their common cause, while another attends similarly to another side. For example, a Young Men's Christian Association may have various sections for sport or reading or politics. The church, however, cannot share in Jesus Christ in her faith or in her work. Wherever she is the church she cannot but will and do everything, or else be no church at all.

The legitimate differences between churches can only be of a technical nature. They are conditioned by differences of time and place, by the fact that we, as children of our time, can in the nature of the case no longer worship God and hear His Word in outward fellowship with the Christians of the fourth century, conditioned too by the fact that the Christians in Aberdeen, for example, cannot in the nature of the case meet together in outward fellowship, as a rule, with those of Edinburgh, much less with those of Basel. But the assembly itself, as an assembly of Christians, is one and undivided, then as to-day, there as here, and is always the same and complete both there and here, then and now. If individual churches unite with one another for joint deliberation, joint speech and action, that, whether it occurs in the narrower confines of a district or country or in œcumenical dimensions, does not mean that the *church* should or could be created thereby for the first time. If the individual churches in their individuality are not already *the church*, then all the churches of the world could unite as closely as they please to form a great union without thereby becoming the church. All that can happen at such a union, be it great or small, is simply that the churches *bear witness to the church* before the world and among themselves, just so far as they are really the church in their own individual existence, i.e. just so far as each of them in her technical difference from the others is at the same time *the church*, and wishes to be nothing but the one complete church

164

in her faith, in her own work and in her relation to other churches. All conferences and all unions—and there are many of them to-day—which do not take place on this basis are so much idle chatter and ado about nothing, which had far better be omitted, because it can only obscure the question of the true nature of the church. This question is put in all seriousness to every individual church and congregation as such and must always be answered by her as an individual church or congregation.

II

Because the church exists in a form manifest to men and therefore in time and in this world, she is nowhere exempted at any time from the possibility of a complete or partial falling away from her head, Jesus Christ, and consequently she is nowhere exempted at any time from the danger of losing her character as the church. She can be and can remain what she is as the church—the assembly founded, sustained and ordered by Jesus Christ. She can be held together and continue so through " the unity of the Spirit in the bond of peace, *one* body, *one* spirit, *one* hope based on the calling, *one* Lord, *one* faith, *one* baptism, *one* God and Father " (Eph. 4, 3), and this unity, thus described, means that she is the one church of Jesus Christ. But she can also lose this unity of hers in Jesus Christ wholly or in part. She can become a society, an institution, set up, protected and utilised by men on their own authority, a piece of work in which, under the title of the service of God, man is openly or secretly concerned with his own glory. This will probably show itself at once in tension and division within the church and in deviation of doctrine and life from the promise and the command, to which a church will hold, if she is *the* church. But this will not always show itself immediately. A church may maintain the external fellowship and tradition and orthodoxy in their entirety and yet cease to be a church. I do not know whether the fathers of the Scottish Confession saw this as clearly as we must see it. But we must see and assert clearly, that the *church* is *always* threatened by the question whether she is the true or the false church, and that perhaps most of all when she thinks most confidently that she is the true church.

This fact brings a necessary unrest into the life of the church and of each church and also into the relation of individual churches to one another. Both the true and the false church exist. No church is ever exempted from the question, "*Am* I the true church?" And no church is exempted from submitting herself to the enquiry of the other churches, "*Art* thou the true church?" This distinction and this question is one which causes unrest and pain, but which may not be suppressed even for the sake of love or peace. We can have no peace with one another or only a hollow peace, where such peace is not our peace in Jesus Christ. Between the true and the false church there can be agreements of one kind or another, tolerance and the like, but not the peace which is our peace in Jesus Christ. It is therefore not merely folly, but downright treason—and this has shown itself more than once in the œcumenical movement—to designate the true and the false church (e.g. the Evangelical Church and the Roman Catholic Church) as parts of the one church of Jesus Christ, as discords which quite well admit of being united in one all-embracing concord to form a harmony. This may hold good when it is a matter of discords on both sides; false churches may meet together very well in such a higher unity, for all false churches do belong together and could form an excellent unity— and it is a point worthy of consideration, whether many a church conference and union has not prospered so well simply because it was a case of a false church that was able to reach a happy understanding and union with another false church. But discord and concord can only disturb and cancel each other. The true and the false church as such admit of no uniting, but are as incompatible as fire and water and woe to him who would deny that. He would thereby only prove that what he considers to be the true church and believes he could unite with other churches is itself the false church, or that he treats the true church as if it too were the false church—and it is just this which is treasonable in such a proceeding. For the true church lives on the truth and in the truth, and truth will not admit of fusion with its contrary, error. The antithesis between the true and the false church is therefore one which must not be ignored, but must be honestly recognised, and that precisely for the sake of love and peace properly understood. The antithesis must be overcome not through the victory of one party over another in a church, or through the victory of one church over another, but through the victory of the truth, through the restoration of the lordship of Jesus Christ in the church. This overcoming of error through the truth is the problem which is raised and must be answered in every age in every church and in the relation of every church to every other. Where this problem did not exist, the church would be eo ipso the false church.

III

The church is engaged in a struggle for *her true nature* as the church. Each church is always faced with the question, does the one, true, holy church exist in her? Does she herself exist as the true church, or is she not perhaps something quite different? May she not be just a piece of venerable tradition fostered by certain families or circles and belonging to the place or land in which she exists? Or is she perhaps just one of the instruments of power of society or of the ruling class in society? The socialists and communists have said so at times. Or is she perhaps just a harmless association to satisfy certain religious needs? Or may she be actually just a shop, in which well-meant morality and " Weltanschauung " of all kinds is offered for sale and disposed of? One feels at times that she is just such a shop, where the wares are cheap and are therefore not held in much honour.

No church exists that has not always to be facing the question whether she is indeed the true church. This holds good both of a great national church or even a world church (even though, like the Roman

Church, it were ever so strongly entrenched in its doctrine and orders) and of a sectarian church (even if its life were ever so deep and animated). There is no church therefore which has not to fight for her existence as the true church. The true church exists in human form, in time, in the course of history, and therefore subject to the temptation to give up her true nature, a temptation which can threaten her at every moment from without or within (or from without *and* within) and which means for the church the danger of becoming a false church. This temptation has to be resisted, and woe to the church which will not resist.

But everything here depends on the resistance being the right resistance (2 Tim. 2, 5). Where and when does that take place? Clearly we must answer, in accordance with all that we have said about the real Christian life, the ordinance governing it and the true Christian life and about the mystery of the church, that this takes place wherever the Holy Spirit is at work in the church. The work of the Holy Spirit is the founding, forming and sustaining of faith in Jesus Christ—a faith which consists in thankfulness and penitence, and which fulfils the law of God by love to God and one's neighbour, and in which we are comforted by the fact that the Son of God has intervened on our behalf. It is God's grace and God's work when men are awakened and called to this faith and are sustained in it. The true church exists where this takes place and only there. Stated in terms of general principles, the church's struggle for her existence can consist simply in the existence of faith and the working of the Holy Spirit in her. The true church exists at the place where this happens. Anything else which might be asserted here is beside the point. The Scottish Confession has enumerated some of the things which at the time of its composition were usually cited as evidence of the true church, and has affixed the necessary question marks. Here it is again speaking in opposition to Roman Catholicism. But there are also non-Catholic churches which would do well to pay attention at this point. In settling this question about the true church, the decisive factor is not the antiquity of the church, as the Confession says (e.g. Cain was older than Abel), nor is it the place (Jerusalem was the city of God and Christ was crucified in it), nor is it succession (for such a succession was to be found in the family of Aaron, which contained ultimately an Annas and a Caiaphas), nor are numbers decisive (the Scribes and Pharisees were more numerous than the disciples of Jesus). And we could continue ourselves—the decisive factor is not the intensity of the piety prevalent in the church (the Pharisees did not fall short in that respect and were Pharisees for all that), nor the beauty of the service (there was no lack of that in Bethel and yet God rejected it through the mouth of Amos), nor her works and sacrifice, nor her morality (it was precisely zeal for that which brought Christ to the Cross), nor the best theology (it never flourished so well as at the time of the destruction of Jerusalem). Why is all this not decisive? Why can a church possess all these advantages and still be a false church? Because all these are advantages according to our own standards, which themselves rest on estimates and valuations of such magnitudes and values as underlie our human judgement. But what makes a church true has nothing to do with any of these magnitudes and values. The true church is distinguished from the false only by the fact that in her Jesus Christ is *present in power*. The true church exists, shines out, fights against temptation and escapes the danger of becoming a false church only where, through the power of Jesus Christ Himself, men enquire about Him, i.e. where they do not care about anything else—success or outward safeguards or about expansion or virtues and wisdom, but about Him and Him alone. Where this question is a burning one, bringing unrest and longing and anger and love, there the true church lives. And there alone ; for this alone is the question asked by faith.

IV

The distinction of the true from the false church is thus always a spiritual distinction, and only as such can it become manifest. This does not mean that the distinction remains invisible. But it does mean that it can only be made by God, and also can only be made visible by Him. It means that this distinction cannot be drawn by us, but can only be recognised by us in faith as one already made by God Himself. The Scottish Confession, like most Reformed Confessions, specifies three points at which this distinction made by God can be seen. Let a man ask, it says, where there is to be found true preaching of the Word of God as witnessed to by the prophets and apostles. Secondly, where are the sacraments as instituted by Jesus Christ rightly administered? Thirdly, where is to be found the ordinance of the church, which is required of us by the Word of God and which means the necessary crisis also among individual men within the church? Note that all these three points—these notae ecclesiae—are of a spiritual nature. All three say, the true church is to be seen where the Holy Spirit of God wills it. For God's Holy Spirit decides where there is true preaching, right administration of the sacraments and faithful accomplishment of this discipline and crisis. And *in what way* God's Holy Spirit decides in these matters, will be seen and known and recognised through faith and so through the Holy Spirit Himself. But God's Holy Spirit speaks and may be heard at the place where He has his dwelling and from which He comes to us, namely, in Jesus Christ as the Word of God. The Holy Spirit is not some unknown fluid which can mean different things at different times, nor is He a magic charm. He is the Spirit of Jesus Christ. What the Reformed Confession means by specifying these three points is that, when we enquire about the true church and consider preaching, the sacraments and the ordinance of the church, it is Jesus Christ Himself as the Word of God, who has to be the subject of our enquiry. We *can* enquire after Him, for He exists in concrete form, as witnessed to in the Bible, in the written word of prophets and apostles. And if we enquire after Him, we shall not remain unanswered. If we measure the life of the church by this standard, it will become clear to us *what* He has founded and sustained as His church and therefore as the true church. And it will also become clear what is the other church, the one that is not His, the false church or the " filthie synagogue " as the Confession calls it. It will become clear, that is, at these three points, whether the church, after whose true nature we are enquiring, is or is not a church *reformed* by Him, that is, a church which He has made subject to Himself. The true church, i.e. the reformed church, is always undergoing this reformation, the reformation, that is, of her preaching, her sacraments and her ordinance by the Word of God. The false church, that is always the unreformed church, was perhaps reformed four hundred years ago, only now to reveal the fact that she is afraid of allowing herself to be further reformed. Faith is necessary, that the church may again and again undergo this reformation by the Word of God, and thus let herself be distinguished as the true church from the false. And faith is necessary in order to see this distinction. What is divine will be done only by God. And that God does what is divine will only be known through God revealing it. But when we have faith like a grain of mustard seed, then the church is undergoing reformation, and when we have faith like a grain of mustard seed we can see this reformation too, and with it the distinction of the true church from the false.

THE GOVERNMENT OF THE CHURCH

(Art. 18*b*-20)

And sik kirks, we the inhabitantis of the Realme of *Scotland*, professoris of *Christ Jesus*, professis our selfis to have in our citties, townes, and places reformed, for the doctrine taucht in our Kirkis, conteined in the writen Worde of God, to wit, in the buiks of the Auld and New Testamentis, in those buikis we meane quhilk of the ancient have been reputed canonicall. In the quhilk we affirme, that all thingis necessary to be beleeved for the salvation of mankinde is sufficiently expressed. The interpretation quhairof, we confesse, neither appertaines to private nor publick persone, nether zit to ony Kirk, for ony preheminence or prerogative, personallie or locallie, quhilk ane hes above ane uther, bot apperteines to the Spirite of God, be the quhilk also the Scripture was written. When controversie then happines, for the right understanding of ony place or sentence of Scripture, or for the reformation of ony abuse within the Kirk of God, we ought not sa meikle to luke what men before us have said or done, as unto that quhilk the halie Ghaist uniformelie speakes within the body of the Scriptures, and unto that quhilk *Christ Jesus* himselfe did, and commanded to be done. For this is ane thing universallie granted, that the Spirite of God, quhilk is the Spirite of unitie, is in nathing contrarious unto himselfe. Gif then the interpretation, determination, or sentence of ony Doctor, Kirk, or Councell, repugne to the plaine Worde of God, written in ony uther place of the Scripture, it is a thing maist certaine, that there is not the true understanding and meaning of the haly Ghaist, although that Councels, Realmes, and Nations have approved and received the same. For we dare non receive or admit ony interpretation quhilk repugnes to ony principall point of our faith, or to ony uther plaine text of Scripture, or zit unto the rule of charitie.

ART. XIX

OF THE AUTHORITIE OF THE SCRIPTURES

As we beleeve and confesse the Scriptures of God sufficient to instruct and make the man of God perfite, so do we affirme and avow the authoritie of the same to be of God, and nether to depend on men nor angelis. We affirme, therefore, that sik as allege the Scripture to have na uther authoritie bot that quhilk it hes received from the Kirk, to be blasphemous against God, and injurious to the trew Kirk, quhilk alwaies heares and obeyis the voice of her awin Spouse and Pastor; bot takis not upon her to be maistres over the samin.

ART. XX

OF GENERALL COUNCELLIS, OF THEIR POWER, AUTHORITIE, AND CAUSE OF THEIR CONVENTION

As we do not rashlie damne that quhilk godly men, assembled togither in generall Councel lawfully gathered, have proponed unto us; so without just examination dare we not receive quhatsoever is obtruded unto men under the name of generall Counçelis : For plaine it is, as they wer men, so have some of them manifestlie erred, and that in matters of great weight and importance. So farre then as the councell previs the determination and commandement that it gives bee the plaine Worde of God, so soone do we reverence and imbrace the same. Bot gif men, under the name of a councel, pretend to forge unto us new artickles of our faith, or to make constitutionis repugning to the Word of God ; then utterlie we must refuse the same as the doctrine of Devils, quhilk drawis our saules from the voyce of our onlie God to follow the doctrines and constitutiones of men. The cause then quhy that generall Councellis convened, was nether to make ony perpetual Law, quhilk God before had not maid, nether zit to forge new Artickles of our beleife, nor to give the Word of God authoritie ; meikle les to make that to be his Word, or zit the trew interpretation of the same, quhilk wes not before be his haly will expressed in his Word : Bot the cause of Councellis (we meane of sik as merite the name of Councellis) wes partlie for confutation of heresies, and for giving publick confession of their faith to the posteritie following, quhilk baith they did by the authoritie of Goddis written Word, and not by ony opinion or prerogative that they culd not erre, be reasson of their generall assemblie : And this we judge to have bene the chiefe cause of general Councellis. The uther wes for gude policie, and ordour to be constitute and observed in the Kirk, quhilk, as in the house of God, it becummis *al things to be done decently and in ordour.* Not that we think that any policie and an ordour in ceremonies can be appoynted for al ages, times, and places : For as ceremonies, sik as men have devised, ar bot temporall ; so may and aucht they to be changed, when they rather foster superstition then that they edifie the Kirk using the same.

I

Who governs the church ? To this question the Scottish Confession gives the clear answer that the church is on no account called, and in no sense qualified, to govern herself. In her human, historical form the church is no less free and alive than she is in the mystery of her Divine Lord. The church may and should speak and act. She may and should make decisions. But in all this the church can only be a servant. She cannot reform herself by her own power, she can only acknowledge the reformation which she undergoes at the hand of her Lord. Her life and her freedom consist in her doing that. Here the Scottish Confession is speaking in contrast to the Roman Catholic system, whose essence consists in the church governing herself by means of an *ecclesiastical order*, represented by the whole body of bishops in their virtual unity with the would-be vicar of Christ, as the holder of what is claimed to be the Apostolic see. But this implies that the Confession has already rejected in advance a modern conception also. This, in distinction from the aristocratic and monarchical idea mentioned above, corresponds somewhat to the democratic idea of the state and looks upon the whole body of believers or the *majority of believers* as the possessors of sovereign power in the church. But the government of the church does not take place through men in either the monarchical or the democratic way. It takes place through the *Word of God*. By the Word of God the Scottish Confession and the whole Reformed church means the *Holy Scriptures* of the Old and New Testaments, in so far as these Scriptures are the concrete form of Jesus Christ, His attestation and explanation through the prophets and apostles, the place where He Himself can be sought and found by any man at any time, the Voice of God's Holy Spirit which can be heard by any man at any time and therefore the source from which faith ever anew draws its knowledge of Jesus Christ and thus its knowledge of God. When the Reformed Confession acknowledges Holy Scripture alone to be the Word of God, it does so not because of some curious partiality for the literature of the Bible, but because of the simple consideration that while both the ancient and modern worlds certainly provide us with good literature of every kind, dealing with what men believed they should feel and think about God and gods, there exists only one testimony to Jesus Christ, in which God Himself has spoken about Himself. According

M   177

to our reading of Article 19 of the Confession it is for this reason that the Scriptures have the authority of God Himself, not because of any human liking or judgement nor because the church considers it correct, but because according to the content of the Scripture it is the case that God Himself has here spoken of Himself. The other literature, ancient and modern, of which we have spoken, may also have religious value for those who think they ought to take an interest in religion. But the church does not take the slightest interest in religion; on the contrary, she takes an interest only in God Himself and in His voice and therefore in human testimony in which the voice of God Himself is to be heard and so in the testimony of the Bible. Consequently it is this testimony alone which the church calls the Word of God. She does not mean by this the book, as a book, or the opinions and lines of thought of its authors; she knows that these men who wrote the Bible were fallible men like all of us. She means by the Word of God Him to Whom this book and this book alone bears testimony. It is in this sense that she says that neither angel nor man, but Holy Scripture alone has the right to possess and exercise sovereign power in the church. The church can and should expound Holy Scripture and by doing so proclaim Jesus Christ. But all exposition is subject to Holy Scripture itself as to a judge who is to be appealed to at all times, in the same way as faith is subject to Jesus Christ as its object and as the church is subject to Him as the mystery of her true nature. Because this is so, neither an ecclesiastical order nor the whole body or the majority of believers can

178

undertake the government of the church. The King's throne is already occupied, and He who occupies it is already in command, and has already undertaken the reformation of the church. Everyone who desires to be more in the church than a servant, His servant, could only be a stranger, desiring to rob the church of her freedom and vitality, and to take her prisoner under the dominion of one of the gods of this world. The church may not listen to the voice of such a stranger or come under the Lordship of a god of this world. He who is great in the church cannot be a ruler, but, whether he holds an office or not, can only be a *servant* of the Divine Word—minister verbi divini.

II

The way taken by the church, the history of the church in time is the history of the exposition of Holy Scripture. Exposition of Scripture is not merely what we understand by the word in its narrower sense, i.e. the direct explanation of the words and substance of the Bible text in the form of commentaries. Preaching, if good preaching, is also exposition, and so is instruction, if it is good instruction. If it were not, it would be bad instruction. The church's special science of dogmatics is also exposition. If it is not, it is bad dogmatics. Morality and art are also exposition. The church's internal and external politics are also exposition. Church history is a long series of variations on the one theme, which is given to it by its charter Holy Scripture, in and with its foundation. The church has, with success or otherwise, constantly had to come to terms with the fact that such is her origin, namely, the testimony of the prophets and apostles. What ensues from constantly coming to terms with this is what forms church history. If the church did not possess this theme, we would have no right to separate her history from the general history of the world and of culture. It is this theme, which raises the history of the church, certainly in the midst of all other history, into prominence in a very definite way, making it special history.

But we must go still further. Who expounds Scripture ? Who is therefore the real subject of church history ? Is it the human commentators, teachers and preachers in the church, even her great heroes of faith, or is it the councils and synods, or is it the infallible Pope or the whole line of the Popes together, or is it the theological faculties, or is it perhaps the religious genius, or perhaps the Christian peoples as such ? The Scottish Confession safeguards itself against all such views and explains that " the interpretation [of Scripture] neither appertaines to private nor publick persone . . . bot apperteines to the Spirite of God, be the quhilk also the scripture was written." In fact, if Scripture as testimony to Jesus Christ is the Word of God, and if it is therefore neither a book of religion nor of magic, whose contents could be mastered and professed by certain men with a gift for such study, who then can expound Scripture but God Himself ? And what can man's exposition of it consist in but once more in an act of service, a faithful and attentive following after the exposition which Scripture desires to give to itself, which Jesus Christ as Lord of Scripture wishes to give to Himself? But if that is so, then church history, i.e. the history of the church's coming to terms with the theme given her in Scripture, cannot primarily be understood as the history of the human opinions, resolutions and actions which have emerged in the course of her coming to terms with her theme. It cannot primarily be understood as the history of the men, whether pious or impious, intelligent or foolish, good or less good, who in the course of the centuries have sought directly or indirectly to under-stand Scripture. Church history must rather be understood primarily as the history of the govern-ment of the church by the Word of God, the history of the exposition of Scripture accomplished by Scripture, i.e. by Jesus Christ Himself in the church. Scriptura scripturae interpres—Scripture is the interpreter of Scripture. Of course we know this self-interpretation of Scripture at all times and in all places only as it is reflected in the human exposition visible in human opinions, resolutions and actions of every kind. But everything depends on our recognising this latter as something secondary, as the reflection of that real and genuine exposition, as the multiplicity of the attempts more or less successful to follow in the steps of that self-exposition of Scripture. That means that church history can never be viewed, presented or judged as church history in the abstract, but always only along with a simultaneous investigation of Scrip-ture and attention to its self-exposition. And where the speech and action of the church of to-day is concerned—and this is especially important—the human

opinions and resolutions which are indispensable here
can never be brought up for discussion in the abstract
as human opinions and resolutions, but the opinion
and the action of the Word of God which governs the
church must be brought up for discussion simul-
taneously—indeed previously when we consider the
matter objectively. There cannot but be a secondary
subject of church history and who else could that be
at any time but man with his human opinions and
resolutions ? But it is just man who must learn to
understand himself not as the primary subject but as
this *secondary* subject ; he must learn to follow, not
to take the initiative. And if he wishes to learn to
think and act as a member of the church—and this
takes a long time to learn—he will have to learn to
think and speak as one who follows after and obeys
the Word of God.

III

What we have just said cannot be understood as
meaning that there cannot or may not be concrete
decisions or obligations in the church. There must
be such decisions and obligations. Where the church
was afraid of forming decisions and obligations she
would not be free or alive, nor would she be serving
her Lord. The Scottish Confession has no intention,
even in Article 20, of denying authority to the Councils
and so to the human instruments for church government generally. The Word of God which governs
the church requires her to justify her actions again
and again to it. The temptation, caused by error, and
the consequent danger that the church could become

a false church, requires her to affirm the truth and deny error. In what other form could this take place than in the shaping of definite human opinions and resolutions ? Every sermon and ultimately every expression of the church's life is as such a decision taking that particular form ; it is a confession. The decrees and explanations of a Council or Synod also can only be decisions taking that particular form— Confessions of Faith. What we hear in them is not a voice speaking from heaven, but only one speaking on earth. None the less they must venture to speak and when they venture to speak by faith they can lay claim to authority. If the church makes a confession of her faith, makes an affirmation in one direction and a denial in another, she is doing something enjoined upon her, not something forbidden. In that case her decision will certainly not lack authority and may count on gaining attention and obedience. The Scottish Confession also is itself such a decision, such a Confession of Faith, made at a time of special confusion in the church, but at a time, too, of special attentiveness to the Word of God which governs the church. And it is obvious that the Confession is not table talk, the mere voicing of opinions, nor edification which imposes no obligation, the expression of nice religious sentiments, nor is it religious journalism. The Confession is speaking under a sense of responsibility and therefore with authority also. But just because the matter concerns it itself, the Scottish Confession has been careful in expressing its opinion as to what authority such a decision by the church can and cannot have. Such a decision or confession of faith, as the Scottish

Confession, cannot under any conditions wish to usurp the place of the Word of God. It cannot claim a validity which is absolute and obligatory for all time. It cannot set up any new doctrine or ordinance which goes beyond the Word of God. Nor can it either diminish or increase the authority of the Word of God, cancel or confirm it, limit it or extend its influence. It cannot bind men's consciences, it is not in principle free from error. It is and remains simply a human decision. If it wished to be more, it would be less, for it would then be a hindrance to the Word of God. In that case it could not be obeyed and its assumed authority would have to be defied in the name of faith, in the name of Jesus Christ. But within its own limits the Confession can be a human decision of such a kind, that through it the way will not be blocked but rather opened up for the Word of God. Through the Word of God itself it can become necessary. It can keep error within its bounds. It can be a worthy sign and instrument to remind future generations also of the truth once known. It can serve the Word of God, not as a law to which faith is subject, but as genuine reiteration of the testimony of the prophets and apostles. In the measure in which it does this, it possesses validity and power. The church cannot profess faith in herself. And her confessions may not be understood or treated as confessions of faith in herself, as the rendering absolute of the piety and the " Weltanschauung " prevailing in her at any given time. This is what happens wherever the Confessions are either over-rated or under-valued. The church in her confessions can profess faith only in her Lord, not in herself, and the church's confessions are to be understood and estimated as confessions of faith in the Lord of the church. If they are conceived in any other way, not with the respect or the freedom thereby given them, but as the law to which faith is subject, then this law may be kept or broken and may be made the object of the idolatry of the orthodox or that of the iconoclasm of the liberals, but in that case the confessions have not yet been understood as the confessions of the church. In that case the orthodox and the liberals can only be asked first of all to cleanse their hands in order that they may make a new beginning in the treatment of this problem. And this new beginning will have to consist in listening with the obedience of faith to what the Fathers have said by faith and to venture to say ourselves in our turn, in the obedience of faith, what one day our children and children's children may hear by faith—i.e. to utter in weak, fallible, human words, humbly but joyfully, a confession of faith in the Word of God.

IV

We shall close with a brief note on the question of *Church government*, mentioned at the beginning. We have established that the government of the church is neither the concern of a particular ecclesiastical order nor that of the whole body or majority of believers. Holy Scripture itself governs the church. The ecclesiastical order *and* the congregation are not lords over it but organs serving it. If this is acknowledged it may now be said for the advancement of peace in this conflict, that within the bounds of this service to Scripture the monarchical mode of government *cannot* have a priority in *principle* over the democratic, or vice versa. It is noteworthy that a good reformed confession like the Scottish Confession has expressed absolutely no opinion on the whole problem of church government. The Reformed churches show a decided preference for a Presbyterian, synodical form of church government. But it would be historically incorrect to say that this is *the* Reformed system of church government. For there are also Reformed churches governed by bishops, e.g. in Hungary. But it is legitimate and necessary none the less to speak of the *relative* superiority of the former system. Jesus Christ is the Lord and Saviour of the congregation as a congregation. It is the congregation, as a congregation, which has to justify its activity to Him. The ecclesiastical order has its life solely in the congregation, but the congregation has not its life solely in the ecclesiastical order. The freedom of the Word of God and the legitimate authority of the decisions and obligations necessary in the church are less menaced where the constitution makes it clear that it is not some few members of the church but all of them who are called and qualified to be vigilant and faithful and, what is more, to be so with equal seriousness, and where the holders of special office have to speak and act only as primi inter pares, joint responsibility being shared by all the rest. Besides, the adherents of an evangelical episcopate have never yet made sufficiently clear what is actually to be understood by the special office of bishop in an evangelical church. I am not aware if they know in Hungary —or in England, or in Sweden, or in Denmark, where there are evangelical bishops. But I am aware that German Lutheranism, which is very keenly episcopal, does not know to this day what it means. There is certainly no reason why we should consider the episcopal solution a better one, but there is also no occasion whatsoever for the friends of a Presbyterian-synodical form of Government to believe this question to be one in which the true nature of the church is at stake. An episcopal church is, as episcopal, to be regretted. But she is not for that reason a false church.

THE CHURCH SERVICE AS DIVINE ACTION

(Art. 21)

ART. XXI

OF THE SACRAMENTIS

As the Fatheris under the Law, besides the veritie of the Sacrifices, had twa chiefe Sacramentes, to wit, Circumcision and the Passeover, the despisers and contemners whereof were not reputed for Gods people ; sa do we acknawledge and confesse that we now in the time of the Evangell have twa chiefe Sacramentes, onelie instituted be the Lord *Jesus*, and commanded to be used of all they that will be reputed members of his body, to wit, Baptisme and the Supper or Table of the Lord *Jesus*, called the Communion of his Body and his Blude. And thir Sacramentes, as weil of Auld as of New Testament, now instituted of God, not onelie to make ane visible difference betwixt his people and they that wes without his league : Bot also to exerce the faith of his Children, and, be participation of the same Sacramentes, to seill in their hearts the assurance of his promise, and of that most blessed conjunction, union and societie, quhilk the elect have with their head *Christ Jesus*. And this we utterlie damne the vanitie of thay that affirme Sacramentes to be nathing ellis bot naked and baire signes. No, wee assuredlie beleeve that be Baptisme we ar ingrafted in *Christ Jesus*, to be made partakers of his justice, be quhilk our sinnes ar covered and remitted. And alswa, that in the Supper richtlie used, *Christ Jesus* is so joined with us, that hee becummis very nurishment and fude of our saules. Not that we imagine anie transubstantiation of bread into *Christes* body, and of wine into his naturall blude, as the *Papistes* have perniciouslie taucht and damnablie beleeved ; bot this unioun and conjunction, quhilk we have with the body and blude of *Christ*

188

Jesus in the richt use of the Sacraments, wrocht be operàtioun of the haly Ghaist, who by trew faith carryis us above al things that are visible, carnal, and earthly, and makes us to feede upon the body and blude of *Christ Jesus*, quhilk wes anes broken and shed for us, quhilk now is in heaven, and appearis in the presence of his Father for us : And zit notwithstanding the far distance of place quhilk is betwixt his body now glorified in heaven and us now mortal in this eird, zit we man assuredly beleve that the bread quhilk wee break, is the communion of *Christes* bodie, and the cupe quhilk we blesse, is the communion of his blude. So that we confesse, and undoubtedlie beleeve, that the faithfull, in the richt use of the Lords Table, do so eat the bodie and drinke the blude of the Lord *Jesus*, that he remaines in them, and they in him : Zea, they are so maid flesh of his flesh, and bone of his bones ; that as the eternall God-head hes given to the flesh of *Christ Jesus* (quhilk of the awin conditioun and nature wes mortal and corruptible) life and immortalitie ; so dois *Christ Jesus* his flesh and blude eattin and drunkin be us, give unto us the same prerogatives. Quhilk, albeit we confesse are nether given unto us at that time onelie, nether zit be the proper power and vertue of the Sacrament onelie ; zit we affirme that the faithfull, in the richt use of the Lords Table, hes conjunctioun with *Christ Jesus*, as the naturall man can not apprehend : Zea, and farther we affirme, that albeit the faithfull, oppressed be negligence and manlie infirmitie, dois not profite sameikle as they wald, in the verie instant action of the Supper ; zit sall it after bring frute furth, as livelie seid sawin in gude ground. For the haly Spirite, quhilk can never be divided fra the richt institution of the Lord *Jesus*, wil not frustrat the faithfull of the fruit of that mysticall action : Bot all thir, we say, cummis of trew faith, quhilk apprehendis *Christ Jesus*, who only makis this Sacrament effectuall unto us. And therefore, whosoever sclanders us, as that we affirme or beleeve Sacraments to be naked and bair Signes, do injurie unto us, and speaks against the manifest trueth. Bot this liberallie and franklie we confesse, that we make ane distinctioun betwixt *Christ Jesus* in his eternall substance, and betwixt the

Elements of the Sacramentall Signes. So that wee will nether worship the Signes, in place of that quhilk is signified be them, nether zit doe we dispise, and interpret them as unprofitable and vaine, bot do use them with all reverence, examining our selves diligentlie before that so we do ; because we are assured be the mouth of the Apostle, *That sik as eat of that bread, and drink of that coup unworthelie, are guiltie of the bodie and blude of* Christ Jesus.

I

According to Reformed teaching, real service of God, and so the life of the church, has its concrete centre in what is usually called the *Church service* in the narrower sense of the word, i.e. the action of the congregation assembled together as such, action which is required and appointed by God and which serves to awaken, purify and advance the Christian life. When the Scottish Confession deals with this subject in Articles 21-23 under the heading " of the Sacramentis," we shall recall that it is engaged in controversy with the conception of the church service which prevailed in the Middle Ages—a conception determined by the sacraments and especially by the Sacrament of the Altar. Over against it the Confession desires to set the right conception of the church service—the one which corresponds to the Word of God. But it is noteworthy that from beginning to end the right conception of the service is expounded from the aspect of the sacraments. Our sixteenth-century forefathers were very far from valuing the sacraments lightly. In opposition to Roman Catholicism they made enquiry about the *true* sacraments. But it must be noted that in doing this they desired to enquire about the *sacraments*, only in a still more serious and fundamental way than their opponents. One might well be astonished that in a document so strictly- reformed as this, at this point the prayers and confession of faith of the congregation are not mentioned at all and preaching only incidentally. What is spoken of here is simply Baptism and the Lord's Supper, and in the main only the Lord's Supper. How the Reformed church has been misunderstood —by herself too as well as by others—when later the impression prevailed that she was a church without sacraments, even a church hostile to the sacraments ! And that, where actually our fathers valued the sacraments so highly that they could hold that the whole of the church service most certainly would and must be right where the teaching and ordering of the sacraments, and especially of the Lord's Supper, were correct. The knowledge which can be perceived behind this historical fact can no longer be entirely strange to us after the course taken hitherto by our lectures. In fact it may well be the case that it is not possible to tackle the problem of the church service in any better way than from this aspect, namely, that of the sacraments.

A sacrament, according to the definitions of the ancient church, which all agree on this matter, and hence according to the Scottish Confession also—a sacrament is an action in which God acts and man serves, his service taking the form of the execution of a divine precept. In accordance with this precept and by means of definite concrete media witness is borne to God's grace and through this men's faith is awakened, purified and advanced. In principle this is all that can be said not only about the sacraments in the narrower sense of the term, but about the *church service* in general. The first point to which we shall give prominence is that the church service is *Divine* action. It is as such that the Scottish Confession has represented it in Article 21, our text in this lecture. We shall have to consider the church service as human action also in our next lecture in connection with Articles 22-23. Note how the vere Deus, vere homo, the whole rhythm of Christian doctrine, with which we are constantly meeting, holds good here also. But here also the vere Deus must come first and condition whatever is to be said about the vere homo. The church service is in the first instance primarily, in origin and in substance, divine action, and is only then human action secondarily, by derivation, and as an accident of the former. What man should and can do here is to serve. And that this service is *divine* service is something which is brought about not by man but by God and God alone. It is *God* who wills that divine service be held. It is *God* who provides the media suitable for it. It is *God* who bears witness through them to His grace. It is *God* who by this means awakens, purifies and advances faith. All along the line it is God not man, and man at every point appears only as the one who serves and who carries out the Will of God.

If we go on from this to ask, first of all, about the reason and purpose of the church service—its *ground*, it must be immediately clear to us, that all that we ourselves can choose and do in it takes second place.

How could the church service but be a practice of *devotion*, a gathering together of thoughts and of hearts around the mystery of the church and of the Christian life, a contemplation of the Grace of God shown forth in Jesus Christ, and a new seeking after Him who has found us in His word. We have need of devotion of this kind. But this is not the primary ground for the church service. Why should it not also mean our *instruction*. Jesus Christ is the Truth, of which we cannot hear enough. Holy Scripture as testimony to Him demands to be expounded and made clear. It is high time that the anti-intellectualism, which has reigned so long in the church, should disappear finally. A service where there is nothing to be learned is not a service at all. We need instruction from God's Word. But this, too, is not the primary ground for the church service. Every service should be a *confession of faith* as well. In the service certain things become visible. We see God's Word being proclaimed and heard. The members of the church become manifest to one another and with this the fact that they belong together becomes visible and thus the church becomes visible as the church. By holding the service we confess our adherence to one another and to the church and to the Word of God. To confess means at least to render visible, and it is necessary that this should come about. But this, too, is not the primary ground for the church service.

The primary ground for the church service lies outside ourselves. It lies in the presence and the action of Jesus Christ. He wishes to rule in mercy

N   193

and faithfulness. He wishes the church to be as He is and to continue as He continues. He wishes to be loved and praised in the Christian life of her members because in His person and in His work He is the meaning and the goal of all human history. It is in the church that this meaning and goal become visible. For this reason He creates and sustains the church, and for this reason and ultimately for this reason alone there is need for the church service. The power possessed by this service consists not in what we desire and do in it, but in the Divine appointment and call which we obey there. The church service is an opus Dei, which takes place for its own sake. This may all seem strange to us and also beneficial to hear. Poor present-day man with his utilitarian notions should certainly find it salutary and comforting to be told once again that there is something which, though it has its utilitarian side too, cannot be founded on utilitarian principles, but has its primary ground in its being *commanded* us. And this thing is the church service.

II

The primary *content* of the church service corresponds to its primary ground. Whatever takes place in it can be concerned only with the execution of the Will and command of the Lord of the church. And His will and command is that the church *exist* and *continue*. The work of the Holy Spirit in the service is to bring this about. And now we have some small understanding of why the Scottish Confession refers at this point only to baptism and the

Lord's Supper, and how far it thinks by doing this it has said all that is necessary to be said here. To what do we find *Baptism* bearing testimony ? That " we ar ingrafted in *Christ Jesus*, to be made partakers of his justice," says the Confession. And to what do we find the *Lord's Supper* bearing testimony ? That " he remains in [us] and [we] in him " because we may enter ever anew into the same fellowship which He as a man of flesh and blood has with the Eternal God. So we see that what we are concerned with in *Baptism* is the church's *existence*. But the church is undergoing reformation. And thus all the emphasis falls now on the *Lord's Supper*. For what we are concerned with in the Lord's Supper is the church's *continuance*. Hence the Divine command embraces, regulates and delimitates the whole church service by Baptism and the Lord's Supper. These form to a certain extent the only necessary sphere of the church service because the only one adequate for it. Whatever takes place in it must have its origin in Baptism, in the *existence* of the church, in the threefold fact that Jesus Christ has once and for all died and risen again for us, that we are irrevocably His and that we are destined for no other end than to be justified, sanctified and glorified through Him. And whatever takes place in the church service must have as its end the *Lord's Supper*, the *continuance* of the church, Jesus Christ's giving us a new share in His existence as man as existence with God and the constant fulfilment of our destiny, which is to be the object of His work. The church service is what takes place between the beginning and the end thus described as testimony to the Grace of God and as the awakening, purifying and advancing of our faith. Therefore the Confession is quite in order in speaking only of Baptism and the Lord's Supper, when it deals with the service.

What lies between these limits? We need now only ask the further question: what must happen when the church of Jesus Christ, assembled by His command, is mindful in the symbol of Baptism of *whence* she *comes*, of her creation through the Word of God? If she is really assembled and if as an assembly she forms a fellowship that must be consummated as a fellowship, and if words must therefore be spoken in this assembly, what words would be possible except those forming the proclamation of God's revelation? The message of God's great act stands at the beginning of all the ways which the church and those within her take, at the outset of their thinking, willing and doing; it is a message which, though it is heard, is never sufficiently heard; it tells, as the conclusion of the Scottish Confession says, that He is risen in all His wrath and in all His mercy, risen in the midst of His enemies to show Himself as God, risen as the Messiah of Israel and as the Son of the Virgin, and risen the third day from the dead. That this is her origin, is a fact about which the church can be under no misapprehension and about which she cannot keep silent. That is the word which must be spoken in her midst and must continue to be spoken : God manifest in Jesus Christ. And the testimony to this, her origin, is Baptism. She can at times forget that this is her origin, and she can misunderstand it or give it a different meaning, but in her midst is Holy

196

Scripture, which refuses to be silent. On the contrary, it speaks of this and nothing else. The Holy Spirit does not let Himself be quenched, and will see to it that the church service must consist constantly in the preaching of the gospel. And now we require only to ask the further question : what must happen when the church of Jesus Christ is mindful in the symbol of the Lord's Supper of *whither* she *goes*, of her preservation through the Word of God ? If she is truly assembled, and if her fellowship must be consummated through words, what can these words be unless the word of faith, which accepts the revelation of God and which is therefore the prayer of thanksgiving, which includes the prayer of repentance and the prayer of praise and all other prayers. The Lord's Supper was called in the ancient church the Eucharist, and as being a Eucharist, a thanksgiving, the Lord's Supper characterises the whole service. The service is faith becoming audible and visible, just as it is the proclamation of revelation. The gratitude which we owe God for His revelation consists in our receiving and accepting Jesus Christ by faith as he exists as man, His body and blood, as the Lord's Supper testifies, in eating and drinking and thus in making Him our own and so in being nourished to this end that we may be with God in Him as He is with God. And it is this too which preserves the church as the true church. We can thank God in no other way than by receiving what He has given us. The Scottish Confession has very wisely and properly noted that in such a thanksgiving the decisive factor is not how much or how little we perceive or experience the partaking of Jesus Christ by faith. In the Lord's Supper what matters much more is the work of the Holy Spirit—a work which is comparable to the sowing of living seed on fruitful ground, and the Holy Spirit is inseparable from the work of Jesus Christ and hence from this sacrament also. In point of fact it is just in connection with the church service that we cannot sufficiently reflect on the fact that faith is something which defies our own lack of faith and disobedience and which must hold fast to God's gracious and Almighty Lordship and care in Jesus Christ and to that alone. Man's faith is always something contrary to his own nature. He must believe that God alone is on his side but that God is really on his side. The church service would be a lost cause if its content were Christian piety and morality and not Christian faith. But the church service is the most important, momentous and majestic thing which can possibly take place on earth, because its primary content is not the work of man but the work of the Holy Spirit and consequently the work of faith.

III

Once more the primary *form* of the church service corresponds to its primary content. In the service revelation and faith have a definite form. Testimony is borne to them in the service by concrete creaturely media, by the human institution of the church, the water of baptism, the bread and wine of the Lord's Supper and the speech and action of the preacher and congregation. In our next lecture we shall have to consider these as human action. But the form also belongs primarily, originally and really to the action of God, and only subsequently, secondarily and in a derivative way to that of man. These concrete, creaturely media are in no sense at the mercy of man's imagination or his likes and dislikes. On the contrary, it is because of God's choice and appointment that just these definite things must happen in the church service. It is *He* who has selected the water, it is *He* who has selected the bread and wine and it is *He* who has selected human words to serve in this way, it is *He* who is the Lord of His creation and of the life of the church. All the human forms found in her life can only be an attempt to do justice to the original form of the church service which is given us in the Word of God. At this point the Scottish Confession had to defend true doctrine and the true ordinance of the Church on two fronts.

Firstly, as over against Catholicism but also as against Lutheranism, it had to draw attention to the fact that the form instituted by God is none the less only the *form* and not the content of the service. The bread which we eat and the cup which we bless is the *communion* of the body and blood of Jesus Christ. These both only are and only do what the creature can be and do here. They point out and characterise, bear testimony and mediate. Through the service they render we eat and drink the true body and blood of Jesus Christ. It is just for that end that they are instituted. Yet in this very function assigned them by God they are not themselves that end for which they serve but as a means. The form of the church

service is appointed by God, but is the creaturely form
and not the divine content. It is not itself revelation
and faith, nor is it in itself the work of the Holy Spirit.
But while the work of the Holy Spirit is taking place,
use is made of this form and it is permitted to serve.
It is as Augustine said the " signum visibile rei invisibilis "—the visibile sign of an invisible thing. The
"res invisibilis" is not without this "signum," but
the " signum visible " is not the " res." Jesus Christ
has not rendered Himself superfluous through the
human institution of the church. Without Jesus
Christ Himself we can do nothing. This is the reformed confession's denial of the realistic doctrine of
the sacrament. Yet one must not for all that miss
the affirmation behind this denial. It is the affirmation made by adoration which seeks God in the highest,
just when He has come right down to us. It is the
affirmation of miracle, of pure miracle which for that
very reason is an admirandum and not a stupendum.
It is the affirmation of God who even in the creation
which serves Him remains Lord alone, the only one
to whom glory is due. For the sake of this affirmation
one should think twice before surrendering the denial
uttered by the reformed church. There are fleshpots
of Egypt to which it were better not to return.

But as against the fanatics and spiritualists of that
time, as of all times—the Scottish Confession had to
draw attention in just as definite a way to the fact that
the form of the church service is *instituted by God*
and therefore not to be separated from its content.
The bread which we eat, the cup which we bless *is* the
communion of the body and blood of Jesus Christ.

Bread and cup are created things and remain so, but through the wisdom and power of God they are instituted to serve, to point out, characterise, testify and mediate. Once again through the service they render, we eat and drink the true body and the true blood of Jesus Christ. It is certainly not with the mouth and the teeth that we do so, but by faith and through the power of the Holy Spirit. Yet we do not do so apart from the service rendered by them, but *through* it. We cannot dispense with the function which it is God's will that they should perform, and therefore we cannot despise or neglect it. They are not nuda signa, mere signs. They are the signs of the divine promise and command. Revelation and faith, the content of the church service, are not its form, but the content is not without the form, without the signum visibile. In the work of the Holy spirit it is precisely of this form that use is made. God has not bound *Himself* but He has bound *us*, as He has a right to do. Jesus Christ has not rendered Himself superfluous, but it is His good pleasure to glorify Himself in the human nature of the church which He has instituted. That is the denial uttered by Reformed doctrine to all idealism and all attempts to escape from the visible church. Here again, if one is to understand the Fathers and the matter at issue correctly, one must note the affirmation contained in the denial. The affirmation applies to the majesty of God which even in the sphere of the creature is majestic in accordance with His good pleasure. It applies to His mercy which by means of His creation gives us occasion and opportunity to praise and magnify

Him. The affirmation applies to the incarnation of the Word, which it is the purpose of the human institution of the church to proclaim. Once again, on account of this affirmation we have every reason to pay heed to the denial expressed by the reformed church on this front too. As soon as we see the church service primarily as divine action, we dare not refuse to see its form also primarily in that light.

THE CHURCH SERVICE AS HUMAN ACTION

(Art. 22-23)

ART. XXII

OF THE RICHT ADMINISTRATIOUN OF THE SACRAMENTIS

That Sacramentis be richtlie ministrat, we judge twa things requisite :
The ane, that they be ministrat be lauchful Ministers, whom we
affirme to be only they that ar appoynted to the preaching of
the word, into quhais mouthes God hes put sum Sermon of
exhortation, they being men lauchfullie chosen thereto be sum
Kirk. The uther, that they be ministrat in sik elements, and
in sik sort, as God hes appointed ; else, we affirme, that they
cease to be the richt Sacraments of *Christ Jesus*. And therefore
it is that we flee the doctrine of the *Papistical* Kirk, in partici-.
patioun of their sacraments ; first, because their Ministers are
na Ministers of *Christ Jesus ;* zea (quhilk is mair horrible)
they suffer wemen, whome the haly Ghaist will not suffer to
teache in the Congregatioun, to baptize : And secundly, because
they have so adulterate both the one Sacrament and the uther
with their awin inventions, that no part of *Christs* action abydes
in the originall puritie : For Oyle, Salt, Spittill, and sik lyke
in Baptisme, ar bot mennis inventiounis. Adoration, Venera-
tion, bearing throw streitis and townes, and keiping of bread
in boxis or buistis, ar prophanatioun of *Christs* Sacramentis,
and na use of the same : For *Christ Jesus* saide, *Take, eat,* &c.,
do ze this in remembrance of me. Be quhilk words and charge
he sanctifyed bread and wine, to the Sacrament of his halie
bodie and blude, to the end that the ane suld be eaten, and that
all suld drinke of the uther, and not that thay suld be keiped
to be worshipped and honoured as God, as the *Papistes* have

done heirtofore. Who also committed Sacrilege, steilling from the people the ane parte of the Sacrament, to wit, the blessed coupe. Moreover, that the Sacramentis be richtly used, it is required, that the end and cause why the Sacramentis were institute, be understanded and observed, asweil of the minister as of the receiveris : For gif the opinion be changed in the receiver, the richt use ceassis ; quhilk is maist evident be the rejection of the sacrifices : As also gif the teacher planely teache fals doctrine, quhilk were odious and abhominable before God (albeit they were his awin ordinance) because that wicked men use them to an uther end than God hes ordaned. The same affirme we of the Sacraments in the *Papistical* kirk ; in quhilk, we affirme, the haill action of the Lord *Jesus* to be adulterated, asweill in the external forme, as in the end and opinion. Quhat *Christ Jesus* did, and commanded to be done, is evident be the Evangelistes and be Saint *Paull :* quhat the Preist dois at his altar we neid not to reheaise. The end and cause of *Chrīsts* institution, and why the selfsame suld be used, is expressed in thir words, *Doe ze this in remembrance of me, als oft as ze sall eit of this bread, and drinke of this coupe, ze sall shaw furth,* that is, extoll, preach, magnifie and praise *the Lords death, till he cum.* Bot to quhat end, and in what opinioun the Preists say their Messe, let the wordes of the same, their awin Doctouris and wrytings witnes : To wit, that they, as Mediatoris betwix *Christ* and his Kirk, do offer unto God the Father, a Sacrifice propitiatorie for the sinnes of the quick and the dead. Quhilk doctrine, as blasphemous to *Christ Jesus,* and making derogation to the sufficiencie of his only Sacrifice, once offered for purgatioun of all they that sall be sanctifyed, we utterly abhorre, detest and renounce.

ART. XXIII

TO WHOME SACRAMENTIS APPERTEINE

We confesse & acknawledge that Baptisme apperteinis asweil to the infants of the faithfull, as unto them that be of age and discretion : And so we damne the error of the *Anabaptists,* who denies baptisme to apperteine to Children, before that they have faith and understanding. Bot the Supper of the Lord, we confesse to apperteine to sik onely as be of the houshald of Faith, and can trie and examine themselves, asweil in their faith, as in their dewtie towards their Nichtbouris ; sik as eite and drink at that haly Table without faith, or being at dissension and division with their brethren, do eat unworthelie : And therefore it is, that in our Kirk our Ministers tak publick & particular examination, of the knawledge and conversation of sik as are to be admitted to the Table of the Lord *Jesus.*

I

Articles 22-23 of our Confession deal with the right administration of the sacraments in the church, or in the general application of this term they deal with what is expected and required of men in the church in regard to the service. In the nature of the case the picture is dominated here more than elsewhere by the historical circumstances in which the Confession had its origin, i.e. the fight against the church of the popes along the main lines of attack then necessary. At that time, when the contrast between mediæval catholicism and the regenerated church became clear, even the most backward man among the people had to take part in the very questions touched on here about how the service ought to be conceived and fashioned by men. For this reason all sorts of details are discussed here, e.g. baptism by a midwife in periculo mortis, the withholding of the cup, the adoration of the host and the mass on the one hand, and on the other the free choice of preachers, the cup for the laity and discipline. Because therefore there are so many details, it is not altogether easy to penetrate to the essential content of what is presented here by the Scottish Church as Reformed doctrine. None the less certain main lines of thought which run through all the details can be established here and when treated freely admit of elucidation with a view to application to the present situation. This we shall try to do now.

Once again we begin by asking after the *ground*—this time after the secondary ground of the church service, and in accordance with what has been established in our last lecture the answer which we constantly receive from our text is that man's part in this matter consists in simple *obedience*. From this point of view the Confession defends the church service against its mediæval deterioration. If we had to model the service by the standards of our religious need and capacity, it would have to have a form quite different from the Reformed one—perhaps the very form of the Roman Catholic mass. And any one with sufficient genius and depth of thought, who uses this latter standard of what is suitable for our religious needs and capabilities to decide what is the right service, will find that whatever he may think at that time will lead him sooner or later back to something not far removed from the Roman mass. The mass in its conception, content and construction is a religious masterpiece. It is the highwater mark in the development of the history of religion and admits of no rival. This achievement should be respected as such. But note that this is the very thing for which the Reformed Confession blames it. Religion with its masterpieces is one thing, Christian faith with its obedience another.

Between the two there is the following important difference, Christian faith is obedience and so its service can only be obedience and not an invention, not even an invention based on profound thought and genius and formed and hallowed by the co-operation of centuries or milleniums. The question we have to answer is not how the service may best correspond to our conceptions of solemnity, beauty, the drama, education, psychology, mystery, etc., or how these points of view are to determine it. Clearly all this was sought for centuries and milleniums in the forming of the Roman Catholic mass—but after all these things do the Gentiles seek. On the contrary, the question we have to answer is how it might best correspond to its primary ground, the gracious will of Jesus Christ present and active in the midst of the Church. Hence we are asked about our obedience, not about our needs and possibilities. It is perfectly in order that the question about the right form of service should never cease to agitate the evangelical churches. It is not true that the right form of service was finally discovered and introduced in the sixteenth century. It is quite in place to ask, whether what is known to us to-day in the Reformed church as the service is really founded on obedience to the Lord of the church, or whether it ought not to have its form changed by the asking of the question as to this its primary ground. But it is by this question alone that one should desire to reform the service. All other standards could lead only to deformation, not reformation, and that is precisely what must not be allowed to occur. The application of such alien standards to bring about reformation always leads to the formation of the false church. Let no man say that it is consideration for the world which surrounds the church, which in the nature of the case calls for the application of such foreign standards. This very consideration requires the opposite. The church would be a bad servant of the world—of the task she has to perform in relation to the world—if out of consideration for the real or assumed desires of the world and its demand for drama, psychology, etc., she desired in her service to be anything but obedient. What the church does owe the world is not her own cleverness or adaptability or the attempt made in all lands at all times to suit the people's wishes, but the gospel of Jesus Christ. And if she considered it more important to be clever than obedient, how could she proclaim the gospel or how would she do it? How could a disobedient church have even the slightest significance for the world? She is a light in the world, the light which according to the promise of her Lord she is to be if she is brave enough to be wiser than the wise and so to hold fast to the Word of her Lord without consideration of the world.

II

For the second time the object of our enquiry is the *content* of the church service; this time we are concerned with its secondary content. The divine action in this matter consists of revelation and faith. We are now enquiring about the corresponding *human* action. It is indeed not unnecessary to stress the fact that the church service is an action, an act, an act of service to the opus Dei, but an act which in itself requires to be performed in the way proper to its subject, just as much as, e.g. a technical, military or political action must be performed in the way proper to its subject. Without any doubt this fact was far clearer to our fathers than it is to us. And because the church cannot die it will have to become clearer to us again also. We spoke in our previous lecture of the fact that it is a matter of the church *existing* through revelation and *continuing* through faith. But this existence and continuance of the church means that what takes place in her is action and not resting or waiting or dreaming or sleep. It is to be noted certainly that this action takes place as an action *of the church*, and consequently in the way proper and peculiar to such action. Some form of activity or other is not enough, not even though it be very well meant and in other connections doubtless thoroughly useful and laudable. The church is neither a charitable institution, nor an institution for the general betterment of the world and man. She is not an institution for the cultivation of fellowship, nor is she a place of intellectual entertainment. The church in modern times has frequently overlooked that and let herself be driven into activity in all these directions, and owing to this she has forgotten and neglected her own proper activity and the reason why she allowed this to happen is simply that she had already forgotten and neglected her own proper action, and wanted, by busily wasting her time, to preserve at least the appearance of active existence in these other activities— a hopeless undertaking. By this means it is indeed not possible to preserve more than the appearance. The content of the church service corresponds to revelation and faith and does not consist in a busy waste of time. In the church to act means *to hear*, i.e. to hear the Word of God, and through the Word of God revelation and faith. It may be objected that this is too small a task and one that is not active enough. But in the whole world there exists no more intense, strenuous or animated action than that which consists in hearing the Word of God—hearing it, as is its due, ever afresh, better, more loyally and efficaciously. Everything beside this is waste of time here. It is in this act that the content of the church service consists. It is because the church hears the Word of God and must hear it again that she preaches, baptises, observes the Lord's Supper and offers thanks. It is as the assembly of those who have heard God's Word and must hear it again that she meets. It is by listening to God that she serves Him. And it is by listening together to God that her members serve one another, as of course they must do. It is by hearing God that the church is built up, lives, grows, works and glorifies God's name in her own midst and in the world. She is the true church in proportion as she is the listening church. Any other goal which she may set herself in general or in detail may bear another name, but can only mean ultimately that the Word of God must be heard. Whatever goes beyond this hearing of God's Word, rests in God's good hands and is His work, not ours. But *we* have this piece of work to do—this is the thing which must be *worked* for and *worked* at in the church—the hearing of God's Word. The question asked of the church service is whether its content consists in this work, whether what happens when her members are assembled together is the hearing of God's Word.

Permit me at this point to make a digression of a practical kind. What we know to-day as the church service both in Roman Catholicism *and* in Protestantism is a torso. The Roman Catholic church has a sacramental service without preaching. But I wish to speak at the moment not for or against her, but about our own Protestant church. We have a service with a sermon but without sacraments. Both types of service are impossible. We saw that Baptism and the Lord's Supper form what we may call the natural bounds of the church service. But these have as a rule disappeared from view in our Protestant service. We do not any longer even realise that a service without sacraments is one which is outwardly incomplete. As a rule we hold such outwardly incomplete services as if it were perfectly natural to do so. What right have we to do that ? We may ask the Roman Catholic church why she celebrates mass without preaching or without proper preaching, but we are asked ourselves what right we have to do what we do. Is there not a pressing danger that by omitting the natural beginning and end of a true service the services we hold are incomplete inwardly and in essence as well ? Would the sermon not be delivered and listened to quite differently and would we not offer thanks during the service quite differently, if everything outwardly and visibly began with baptism and moved towards the Lord's Supper ? Why do the numerous movements and attempts to bring the liturgy of the Reformed church up to date—attempts and movements much spoken about all over the world to-day—prove without exception so unfruitful ? Is it not just because they do not fix their attention on this fundamental defect, the incompleteness of our usual service, i.e. its lack of sacraments ? * In these circumstances what force can our criticism of the opposite defect in the Roman Catholic service have ? I mention this in this context for the following reasons. The hearing of the Word of God forms the real action of the church and in the last resort everything depends on its taking place around the centre characterised by the two sacraments. When we hear that everything has been accomplished for us in Jesus Christ and that we have everything to expect from Him, we are hearing the Word of God then and are consequently good labourers in God's vineyard. But do we hear that all this is true ? And if for a long time we have not been hearing it in our Protestant churches either as we should and ought to have heard it, if to a great extent the sermon has not been delivered and heard as it should be and men have not given thanks in the way they should, is not all this bound up perhaps with the fundamental defect of our service, that the almost complete disappearance of the sacraments has left the service a torso ?

We shall close our section on the content of the church service by showing that the promise and the responsibility attaching to the action, to which the

* Proposals for the playing of a violin or for the singing of solos, or for all repeating prayers together are very nice, but they do not really help here.

congregation is called, concerns both the holders of ecclesiastical office and the remaining members of the congregation equally seriously and ultimately in common. No one is released from the task of hearing the Word of God, and in that task no one has a less important part than the others. All are hearers of the Divine Word, and for that very reason all are also priests. In the church there are no clergy and no laymen. The distinction between the holders of a special office and the remaining members of the congregation, between the teaching church and the hearing church—the ecclesia docens and the ecclesia audiens—can be only a technical distinction and not one of principle. For the words uttered by certain members are simply the transition from hearing to further hearing of God's Word, and the speakers, because they, too, are listening, effect this transition in common with those who are primarily only hearers. Only primarily, however. In the service the speaking as such is the concern of some and not of others, and this is a parable which may not be set aside—a parable of the fact that God speaks but it is man's task to listen. Yet the singing with which the other members of the congregation respond is equally a parable of the fact that the voice of thanksgiving for God's revelation must be the voice of the whole church, and the sermon, too, is a part of such thanksgiving. And in a living church the whole congregation must have a share in one way or another, directly or indirectly, in the special promise and responsibility attaching to teaching, which is itself simply one function in the common task of hearing God's Word.

III

If the content of the church service is the hearing of the Word of God, then the last question to which we now come has also already been settled. The question runs, what is the secondary *form* of the church service ? What can and should take place on man's side in consequence of God on His side having given man the definite media, signs and testimonies already mentioned, through the use of which man is to become and be and become again and again an obedient hearer of the Word of God ? We have seen that in connection with the form of the church service also we are not left to ourselves, our own imagination and arbitrary choice, but are shown definite paths to take. And we must take these paths. The water of baptism, the bread and wine of the Lord's Supper and the words of Scripture are to be received not as ordinary water, ordinary nourishment and ordinary words, but as water, nourishment and words which bear a testimony.

Thus on man's side what must be done is to *enquire* after the institution of the church as established by Jesus Christ, and this enquiry must be continuous, scrutinising and discriminating. This institution is certainly given us by Him, but it is to be recognised and acknowledged by us ourselves. Hence the hearing of the Word of God which is mediated to us through that institution and the action of the church which takes place on the basis of the institution cannot consist in an opus operatum but in a proclamation and perception of God's Word, which is *qualified* not unqualified. It must be done with

214

sincerity and with *humility ;* with sincerity because it must be open to the truth of God's Word and with humility because it must be ready to bow in the presence of the superiority of that Word. Otherwise, if we are not sincere and humble, we are not taking the way, though it has been shown us and prescribed for us. Otherwise all proclamation and perception is in vain and otherwise we do not really hear. We are not hearers of God's Word as a matter of course, nor are we sincere and humble as a matter of course. This necessary secondary form of the church service is given us rather as a *task*, a task which consists in an effort of a critical nature which we may neither evade nor allow to lapse. In this connection the Scottish Confession imposed strict requirements both on the preachers and the remaining members of the church. If this effort does not take place, we would be receiving only ordinary water, nourishment and words, not the water, nourishment and words which bear a testimony. It is certainly primarily the work of the Holy Spirit, which enables us to receive the latter. But His work does not come about without the corresponding critical effort on our side. We may observe now that this effort of criticism, scrutiny and discrimination, all things considered, is nothing else than *theology.* What theology does is to ask questions, and without this the church would get no answers. It is only on the human side that theology has this significance. Hence it can neither take the place of, nor supplement the work of the Holy Spirit. And even on the human side it has only this formal significance. It can neither take the place of nor supplement the church's hearing of the Word of God, as the real human act in the church service. It has a very modest significance, but it has this significance, and therefore it causes unrest and often for this reason the church shuts its ears to theology. It enquires if our hearing of God's Word is being duly qualified and it enquires about the adequacy of our proclamation and perception in relation to the institution of the church as established by Jesus Christ. It asks the church about her sincerity and humility. To this extent theology, too, belongs to the church service and is itself a leaven for the church's liturgy. And to this extent it must be admitted, too, that the church service is necessarily a theological act. May we be able to say of it that it is the act of a good and true theology! But what is a good or a true theology? Are we to follow the teaching of one professor or another here? In a word, every theology is good and true when it is critical, i.e. when it gives expression to the criticism passed by the Lord of the church and hence by Scripture, because it itself is sincerely and humbly subject to the criticism passed by the Lord of the church and hence by Scripture. A bad theology would be one which in this respect was uncritical.

LECTURE XIX

THE STATE'S SERVICE OF GOD

(Art. 24)

ART. XXIV

OF THE CIVILE MAGISTRATE

We confesse and acknawledge Empyres, Kingdomes, Dominiounis, and Citties to be distincted and ordained be God ; the powers and authoritie in the same, be it of Emperours in their Empyres, of Kingis in their Realmes, Dukes and Princes in their Dominionis, and of utheris Magistrates in the Citties, to be Gods haly ordinance, ordained for manifestatioun of his awin glory, and for the singular profite and commoditie of mankind : So that whosoever goeth about to take away, or to confound the haill state of Civile policies, now long established ; we affirme the same men not onely to be enimies to mankinde, but also wickedly to fecht against Goddis expressed will. Wee farther confesse and acknawledge, that sik persouns as are placed in authoritie ar to be loved, honoured, feared, and halden in most reverent estimatioun ; because that they are the Lieu-tennents of God, in whose Sessiouns God himself dois sit and judge : Zea, even the Judges & Princes themselves, to whome be God is given the sword, to the praise and defence of gude men, and to revenge and punish all open malefactors. Mairover, to Kings, Princes, Rulers and Magistrates, wee affirme that chieflie and most principallie the conservation and purgation of the Religioun apperteinis ; so that not onlie they are appointed for Civill policie, bot also for maintenance of the trew Religioun, and for suppressing of Idolatrie and Superstitioun whatsoever : As in *David, Josaphat, Ezechias, Josias*, and utheris highlie commended for their zeale in that caise, may be espyed.

And therefore wee confesse and avow, that sik as resist the supreme power, doing that thing quhilk appertains to his charge, do resist Goddis ordinance ; and therefore cannot be guiltles. And farther we affirme, that whosoever denies unto them ayde, their counsell and comfort, quhiles the Princes and Rulers vigilantly travell in execution of their office, that the same men deny their helpe, support and counsell to God, quha, be the presence of his Lieu-tennent, dois crave it of them.

I

The title which I have given to the subject-matter of Article 24 of the Scottish Confession, " The State's Service of God," sounds unusual and artificial. But when I consider both the context and the content of this article and the matter itself, I do not know any other way in which I could express myself. Reformed doctrine does not merely know the service of God rendered by the Christian life, and the church service in the narrower sense of the term, with which we have been occupied in the last two lectures. On a third level of thought and reality, it knows also a service of God *rendered by the State*. We shall be able to see this third level, once we reflect that the Christian life and the life of the church are enacted within the confines of a *world* which does *not yet* listen to the Word of God, which is still a stranger to the Lordship and judgement of Jesus Christ and which therefore cannot yet be claimed to be under the obedience of faith. Note that the Christians, too, belong to this world, even when church members and conscious and active members, in so far as it is true to say of them, too, that they are not yet under the obedience of faith, but are still constantly engaged in the conflict of the flesh with the spirit, a conflict in which the church herself is engaged in and with her members. What is to become of the world—and of the church in so far as she, too, is still in the world, belongs to the world and is herself worldly ? The decisive answer must certainly be that the world may and must *hear the Word of God.* The world is the object of the church's mission, though the church will frankly own here that she herself is the very first to need the mission work which she has to perform. But the church by the very act of performing her mission towards the world—in principle the one and only thing which she can do for it—does thereby achieve to some extent an *anticipation* of what is to come. The existence of the church in the world, the fact that she must venture to speak the Word of God to it, means a *sanctification* of the world, preliminary but none the less real. It is *preliminary* because it is not to be confounded with the sanctification which can come about only when the world listens to God's Word, permits itself to be called to faith, and so becomes itself the church. But it is none the less *real*, a work of the Holy Spirit's, just as truly as the other is, but at present applied only externally and connected with the whole sphere of what is not yet under the obedience of faith. This sphere is in reality not yet the sphere of the Christian life or of the church. Here the argument of Article 24 is directed against those sixteenth-century movements, which overlooked this fact that the world is not yet under the obedience of faith, and which therefore thought that they could set up the kingdom of the Saints in cities and countries and that they ought to do so. What we are dealing with here are tasks other

than that, and preliminary and subordinate to it.
But neither is it true that Jesus Christ is not yet the
Lord and moreover the only Lord and Judge in this
sphere also. He is Lord and Judge manifestly, when
the Word of God enters this sphere by its proclamation,
and when faith in Him is confessed here. But he is
present, too, secretly, wherever such proclamation and
confession of faith is not yet to be heard. Wherever
God's Word is proclaimed and confession of faith in
Jesus Christ is made, there will certainly be proclamation and confession of the fact that His Kingdom
has no end and that in this external sphere too there
exists no law, truth or reality which can set bounds
to the Church's task or can set aside or even check
faith active in love. Thus in such places the anticipation referred to is of necessity brought about. And
the world with its claim to be merely the world
and to be its own law-giver is not taken seriously—
either in the sense that it should be left to its own devices in its indifference or in its indignation, or in the
sense that it should be granted a charter, under which
it would be permitted to lead a life of independence.
Here, too, Article 24 is directed against those sixteenth-
century movements, which wished to urge the Christian
to have no interest in the world, but to withdraw from
it, and it is directed against those, which, like Lutheranism, wish to combine withdrawal from the world with
the acknowledgement of a certain independence of
the Kingdom of the world over against the Kingdom
of Jesus Christ. According to Reformed teaching
neither attitude is true—withdrawal from the world
or recognition of the independence of the world ;

these two realms are indeed to be distinguished, but are none the less one, in so far as Jesus Christ is Lord not only of the church but also of the world. He is the Lord of the world in that quite different way mentioned above, in the form of the claim to the political order which He makes. Consequently the claim which that order imposes on every man is founded not on a special law governing the world, but on God's law, which is proclaimed in the church and holds good for the world also. It is founded " as God's haly ordinance," and just to this extent it has a real and true foundation. The political order is not only of service for " the singular profite and commoditie of mankind." On the contrary, it also serves " for manifestatioun of God's awin glory " and is, just to this extent, a real and beneficial ordering of human life as well. It is not yet the order of faith and love, but, as it were, the shadow which that order casts before it—the order of outward justice, outward peace and outward freedom. It is not yet the order of inward, spiritual justice and peace, nor yet the order of the freedom of the children of God. It is certainly not yet God's eternal Kingdom but is the promise of this latter in the midst of the chaos of the Kingdom of the world. That is the sanctification of the world through the existence of the church. That is the anticipation of what is to come, which the church brings about in relation to the world by proclaiming to it the Word of God. The church claims the order governing the world also, the political order as an order *for the service of God*. She claims it, that is, as an order, in which rulers and ruled are summoned to obedience to God and hence to thankfulness and penitence in the special, preliminary and preparatory way appropriate to this sphere of what is not yet under the obedience of faith. Only outward justice, outward peace and outward freedom can be brought about and preserved here and that only when recourse is made to physical force. What we are concerned with here can be only a sign pointing to life in Jesus Christ as the life of faith and love. But it is under these very conditions that God commands us to bring about such justice, peace and freedom and to preserve it. Therefore in these conditions there does exist a service of God in the *world* also, a service of God *rendered by the State.*

II

We have seen, throughout the second part of our lectures, how the Christian life and the life of the church is in a state of crisis brought upon it by the question about the *true* service of God, and by the question about the *true* nature of the Christian life and of the church. We have seen how every individual and thus also the church as a whole would be lost if Jesus Christ did not answer this question ever anew in their favour. And we have seen how this question none the less means for the men in the church also a problem which is continually raised and a task which must never be neglected. We can have no cause for surprise if a corresponding statement must be made about the service of God *rendered by the State,* which is to some degree co-ordinate with the life of Christians and of the church. The political order is from time to time in the hands of definite political *powers and rulers*. Paul makes use of an expression which is clearly sacred and not profane, when in Romans 13, 6 he describes these rulers as ministers of God (λειτουργόι) who are ordained of God to the administration of the political order (Rom. 13, 1). They are manifestly ordained to their position in precisely the same way as the church and her members are ordained of God as the assembly of believers for the proclaiming and hearing of the Word of God. But just as the church is constantly asked if she is what her name signifies, so also the same question is put even more insistently to the State, to the political order in the concrete form in which it is administered by specific political rulers. That it is ordained of God protects the State from this question just as little as it protects the church. The political order stands or falls with the Grace of God and here again that does not preclude but involves its being something which must be constantly sought and found by men. Its *significance as service of God* can be *clear* in one place and *obscure* in another.

It does not become clear by rulers professing the Christian faith and indeed being known as men who personally are sincerely pious. When this is the case, one can rejoice at it for their sakes, and perhaps for the sake of the church also. But that in itself does not make clear the significance of the political order as service of God. That significance was often very obscure where one would have thought it could have been seen most clearly, in view of the acknowledged

Christianity of the rulers in question. And conversely it does not necessarily become obscured through rulers having no church connection or at most a doubtful one, though we may be sorry for that for their sakes. Rather under certain circumstances this significance can become very clear even then, clearer in' fact than where the State seems to have a very Christian appearance.

The question here is rather the very simple one, as to what the authority in question *wills and does*. It is thus that the question has been put in the Scottish Confession. Does the political power—this king or that magistrate—do what it is its business to do? Does it abide by God's commandments? Does it remain within the bounds of justice and within the bounds of its task? Does it therefore, by showing this attitude, possess legitimate " authoritie " ? That is the question. Is it not one which can and must be raised constantly in connection with every political power? This question is certainly asked by God. The other alternative could also come about ; the holders of political power could fail to do their duty. They could violate and destroy the justice, freedom and peace which they ought to safeguard. Their power could become tyranny, as is explicitly stated in Article 14, and they could in one way or another fail to display any legitimate " authoritie." In such a case the significance of the political order as service of God becomes manifestly obscured, ceases to be credible, indeed, becomes a mockery, and is made a mockery by the very people who administer it and who are ordained of God. What significance has it now that they are ordained of God, that God sits in their sessions and that they claim His authority? Even though all these things remain the same, it has clearly quite a different significance from the previous case, where the political powers make clear what they now make obscure by their actions. Just because there is no alteration in the Divine appointment of the political order, it is now manifestly true that " God Himself dois . . . judge even the judges themselves " and that the sword they wield is turned against themselves.

And now the Scottish Confession has rightly raised a second question alongside the first one. The second question, however, ought to be formulated somewhat more exactly and more carefully than has been done by the Confession. The Confession maintains that the right use of political power will show itself unambiguously in its administration in relation to the *church*. This is to go too far. Indeed a certain theological error is involved in the demand made of the State, that it should not merely defend the true church but that in a given case it should also undertake the reformation of the church and therefore the restoration of the true church and in this way follow the example of the Old Testament kings in suppressing all idolatry and all superstition which arises in the church. To maintain this is to go too far and indeed to do so in a way that is dangerous. Spiritual perversity must be overcome with spiritual force and not with political. If the church fails to recognise that, who is going to guarantee what reformations may one day be demanded of her by means of political force by some Josiah or other? If this view were true, Hitler would be right in his attempt to reform the church. But fortunately it is not the task of the State to reform the church. But it is correct to say that the significance of the political order as service of God becomes clear where the State provides and preserves *freedom* for the church. The church requires nothing more and declines anything further. But she does require full freedom to pursue her own task, which is a different one from that of the State. Forgiveness of sin is something different from justice. And eternal life is not the same as peace and freedom. The church requires scope to deliver *her own* message about forgiveness of sins and eternal life in the name of her Lord. The significance of the political order as the service of God is obscured where the State refuses the church this scope or sets limits to it. It is obscured where the State demands of the church that she subject and adapt herself to the aims of the State. It is obscured when the State furthers the false church in opposition to the true. It is obscured where the State, perhaps by making its own aims absolute, as in Germany to-day, becomes itself a church, a church which will without doubt be a false one and the most intolerant of all churches. The question then which the State cannot evade is : does it make clear or obscure the significance of the political order as service of God ? Is it on the way to becoming in its sphere what Romans 13 calls God's representative and priest or is it on the way to becoming the beast rising up out of the sea of Revelation 13 ? It is either one or the other.

III

The answer which is given to the previous question determines the attitude which we are required to take up within the political order. I say explicitly *within* the political order. The political order qua political order and the necessity for it is not something open to question, whatever the conduct of the political power may be. And the significance of the political order as service of God is not affected by its being made clear at one point and obscured at another. Consequently our attitude under all conditions can only be an attitude within this order. But when the significance of this order is clear, the attitude which we take up within it will be different from the one which we take up when it is not clear.

There is no universally valid demand whose purport is that we should have to put our *positive co-operation* at the disposal of the political powers in the tasks and aims which are for the moment theirs. The Scottish Confession has rightly drawn a very clear distinction here between lawful and unlawful authority. We can afford the State such positive co-operation only when the significance of the State as service of God is made clear and credible to us by the State itself, by its attitude and acts, its intervening on behalf of justice, peace and freedom and its conduct towards the church. That is the condition which the *Confessio Scotica* is right in constantly laying down. If that condition is not fulfilled, then, to speak for the moment in general terms, we can only endure in the same way as we must endure other evil forces which we cannot avert. The

227

significance of the political order as service of God remains, even when those who administer it make it a mockery. But in that case we can take no share in their responsibility, we cannot further their intentions, we cannot wish to strive with them to attain their aims. We cannot do it under any conditions or on any pretext. We have to put to ourselves the question mentioned above. And it means a responsible decision of faith and love, when we venture in point of fact to take up an active position within the political order, and not *merely* endure it.

But neither have we a universally valid duty nor even indeed a universally valid right to *refuse* the State our positive co-operation and our participation in its responsibility. We would have the duty to refuse this if the character of the political order as service of God were in fact made obscure to us. But —and on this point the Scottish Confession is perfectly plain—we have not even the right to refuse this, so long and so far as this character of the political order is made clear to us in concreto. In that case our duty is to co-operate with the political power. We are then bound to put our assistance and ourselves at the disposal of the State for the carrying out of its service. If in that case we were to refuse to do our duty as citizens, we should be denying God just as much as if we were to disavow our Confession in the church. Once again we are faced with the question mentioned above. And once again it means a responsible decision of faith and love, should we really venture to adopt the other, the passive attitude within the political order.

IV

There is a particular passage in Article 14 of the Confession, in its exposition of the sixth Commandment, to which we must now return and which compels us to go one step further in this connection. It is explicitly stated there that to the fulfilment of the commandment " Thou shalt not kill " belongs also the command " to represse tyrannie " and not to allow the shedding of innocent blood when we can prevent it. What does this mean ? It means that, according to the Scottish Confession, under certain conditions there may be a *resistance* to the political power, which is not merely allowed but enjoined by God. John Knox and his friends have supplied the unambiguous commentary to this by their words and deeds. This may be not only a passive resistance but an *active* one, a resistance which can in certain circumstances be a matter of opposing *force* by force, as did occur in Scotland in the sixteenth century. It may be that the repressing of tyranny and the prevention of the shedding of innocent blood can be carried out in no other way.

What are we to say to this ? I think, all things being considered, we must agree with the Confession here. We certainly cannot escape obedience to God and to the political order. Nor can we evade praying in accordance with 1 Timothy 2, 1-4 for those who administer that order, whoever they may be and however they may do it. This prayer and this obedience may not cease, no matter whether the significance of the political order be clear or obscure. But in certain circumstances the form which this obedience and prayer take as regards the actual administrators and representatives of the political power, may be not that of the active or passive position mentioned above but a third alternative. Obedience not to the political order, but to its actual representatives can become impossible for us, if we wish at the same time to hold fast to faith and love. It could well be that we could obey specific rulers only by being disobedient to God, and by being thus in fact disobedient to the political order ordained of God as well. It could well be that we had to do with a Government of liars, murderers and incendiaries, with a Government which wished to usurp the place of God, to fetter the conscience, to suppress the church and become itself the Church of Antichrist. It would be clear in such a case that we could only choose either to obey this Government by disobeying God or to obey God by disobeying this Government. In such a case must not God be obeyed rather than men? Must it not be forbidden us then to desire merely to endure? In such a case must not faith in Jesus Christ active in love necessitate our active resistance in just the same way as it necessitates passive resistance or our positive co-operation, when we are not faced with this choice? Must it not necessitate this in precisely the same way as in corresponding circumstances it necessitates reformation and therefore a breach in the church, the breach between the true and the false church? Must not the prayer for this Government, without ceasing to be intercession for them personally before God, for their conversion and their eternal salvation become quite plainly the prayer that as political rulers they may be set aside ? And in such a case would we not have to act in accordance with our prayer ? Against this it may be asked, can we and have we the right as Christians to take part in the use of force in certain circumstances ? This question recalls once again the position with which we began the whole subject in this chapter. We are here as we deal with church and State, so to speak, on the edge of the church in the sphere of the world not yet redeemed. To live in this world and to obey God in it is to take part in the use of force directly or indirectly. It is not first of all in connection with this last case of active resistance to definite powers that the question of force arises.

Let us be quite clear ; by obeying the political order in accordance with God's command, we have in any case directly or indirectly a share in the exercise of force. We have a share in this even when we feel it is our duty to choose that middle way of passive participation. And whether the repressing of tyranny will be a matter of forcible resistance or not, is not something which can be decided in advance. But active resistance as such cannot and may not be excluded out of fear of the ultima ratio of forcible resistance. And the possible consequence of forcible resistance may certainly not be excluded in advance.

We may and should pray to be spared that choice. or, if that be not possible, at least to be spared the ultima ratio of forcible resistance. And we should and must examine our responsibilities here, indeed, if possible, even more carefully than in the decisions previously mentioned. But there is one thing which must not happen. We may neither pray nor wish to be spared obedience to God in this worldly sphere either, to be spared the political service of God as such. And since we now have been claimed for it we may not take flight from any of its consequences demanded of us. The world needs men and it would be sad if it were just the Christians who did not wish to be men.

THE GIFT OF COMFORT AND HOPE

(Art. 25*b*)

ART. XXV*b*

Bot sik as with heart unfainedly beleeve, and with mouth bauldly confesse the Lord *Jesus*, as before we have said, sall most assuredly receive their guiftes : First, in this life, remission of sinnes, and that be only faith in *Christs* blude ; in samekle, that albeit sinne remaine and continuallie abyde in thir our mortall bodies, zit it is not imputed unto us, bot is remitted, and covered with *Christs* Justice. Secundly, in the general Judgement, there sall be given to every man and woman resurrection of the flesh : For the Sea sall give her dead ; the Earth, they that therein be inclosed ; zea, the Eternall our God sall stretche out his hand on the dust, and the dead sall arise uncorruptible, and that in the substance of the selfe same flesh that every man now beiris, to receive according to their warkis, glory or punishment : For sik as now delyte in vanity, cruelty, filthynes, superstition or Idolatry, sal be adjudged to the fire unquencheable : In quhilk they sall be tormented for ever, asweill in their awin bodyes, as in their saules, quhilk now they give to serve the Devill in all abhomination. Bot sik as continew in weil doing to the end, bauldely professing the Lord *Jesus*, we constantly beleve, that they sall receive glorie, honor, and immortality, to reigne for ever in life everlasting with *Christ Jesus*, to whose glorified body all his Elect sall be made lyke, when he sall appeir againe in judgement, and sall rander up the kingdome to God his Father, who then sall bee, and ever sall remaine all in all things God blessed for ever : To whome, with the Sonne and with the haly Ghaist, be all honour and glorie, now and ever. *So be it.*

Arise (O Lord) and let thy enimies be confounded ; let them flee from thy presence that hate thy godlie Name. Give thy servands strenth to speake thy word in bauldnesse, and let all Natiouns cleave to thy trew knawledge. Amen.

I

The first third of this, the 25th and last article of the Confession (i.e. up to the words " and therefore have they na fruite of *Christs* death, Resurrection nor Ascension "), has already been dealt with in our 14th lecture. What is said there, from the nature of its content, belongs somewhere halfway between Articles 16 and 17. That it is said here and not at that place may well be one of the traces of the somewhat hasty editing which is characteristic of the whole document.* If we had to do with a passage out of the Old or New Testaments, the ingenuity of higher criticism would not fail to raise doubts whether misunderstanding on the part of a scribe has not caused a dislocation of the pages here. But it must none the less be noted, that the further reminder of the ambiguous character of the historical form of the church can, in connection with what follows, be to some purpose even here. Despite all reformation the true church and the false are at present still together, just as the wheat and the tares are together and just as according to Article 13 the flesh and the spirit in the Christian life despite all the struggle are still together. The church is looking forward to a final eternal *judgement*,

* As Prof. G. D. Henderson has shown in his introduction to the new edition of the Confession.

in which the separation of the two will be accomplished and the true church will be made unmistakeably visible. This judgement, which for the present remains hidden, will be the church's justification.

What this means can perhaps be shown even more clearly, if we proceed from the results of our last lecture on the political service of God. We considered the life of the church in its necessary relation to that of the State, and we considered the Christian life in its necessary determination as political duty and responsibility. This relation and this determination can neither be denied nor avoided ; there is no escape from them. The life of faith is enacted in this world. The believer belongs to this world with every word that he speaks and with every step that he takes. If he sought to think even for a moment that he was outside the world, he would only be giving way to fancy. But the order governing the world—so far as the world is ordered at all, and in many ways it is in disorder—is the political order. And this very order, even in its best forms, is a questionable one. What it can bring about and preserve is outward justice, outward freedom and outward peace. Behind these a whole slough of injustice, bondage and strife lies hidden. We are not yet in the Kingdom of God. This is manifestly shown by the fact that this order cannot be preserved even in its best forms save by means of *force* and *coercion*. And once again, force and coercion threaten to become more indispensable than ever, when it is a case of replacing a worse form of this order by a better. But love in which faith has its life—and with it faith itself—is clearly endangered where we have to have recourse to force and coercion as means. This danger does not first arise with the possibility of revolution against some definitely bad form of the political order. On the contrary, it arises with the " normal " attitude of submission to what may conceivably be the best form of that order. Even in such a case we give our assent directly or indirectly to force and coercion. Let us recall a single fact: the life of the State, whose character as service of God should be perfectly clear to us, must hold itself ready to make *war*, and we ourselves are involved by it in this readiness, and perhaps sooner or later in something more than readiness ! What will become of faith and love then ? We are not going to say that one can in no circumstances take part in war in faith and love. But there are cogent reasons for maintaining that war—and not only war but the whole atmosphere of force and coercion characteristic of the political life critically endangers faith and love. Does the use of such means not involve our leaving the service of Jesus Christ and our entering the service of other masters ? That is the questionableness and the danger of the State's service of God.

If both the necessity of the State's service of God *and* its questionableness and danger cannot escape our notice, then we cannot fail to notice either the fact that this proclaims, that even the church and even the Christians live here and now within the confines of a world not yet redeemed, and that this world is the world of sinful man, whose reconciliation is indeed *already accomplished* in Jesus Christ but is *still hidden.* What was done for man once and for all on Calvary and what his life is in the mystery of God to all eternity is one thing, and what he himself experiences, thinks and does here and now is another. The Word of God and faith are the bridge between the one and the other. But the gulf between the two remains, and this bridge over it is formed only by the Word of God and faith. Hence our existence in the church *and* in the State, with all the problems which surround this twofold existence. Hence, too, the ambiguous form of the church herself. Hence life in the spirit *and* in the flesh, in the struggle of the one against the other. And hence the judgement, the day of the Lord, as the goal and the end of all, even of all our days as Christian men.

II

It is noteworthy that the heading of this last article is not " of the last judgement," but " of the guiftes freely given to the Kirk." In accordance with the content of the article, I have entitled this chapter— The Gift of Comfort and Hope. Our forefathers did not overlook the enigmatic character of the life of the church and of Christians. In fact in the very face of this enigma they held fast to the gift which has been vouchsafed and promised to the church by God. And in the divine judgement itself, which is to come and which will solve this enigma finally and for ever, they saw the gift of God and not something for fear and trembling. They looked forward with gladness to the judgement. That is the final lesson which we have to learn from them.

To sum up : the discord in the existence of the church and in that of the Christian is to be seen and acknowledged as such. The church would not be alive if she failed courageously to enter into this discord. Nor would she be alive if she did not perceive it as discord and did not suffer under it. And once more the church would not be alive if she thought that she could overcome this discord by means of anything which could be felt, thought, said or done by Christians. There are systems enough whose purport is to endow the church and Christians with strength and confidence for their existence in the world by giving them advice of one kind or another on how to be done with the riddle and contradiction of their existence, and on how to gain peace from the menace to their existence. There are conservative systems, which maintain that in order to master that enigma, the church has internally only to consolidate herself as far as possible and externally to enter into the most reliable agreements she can with State and people, society and learning. And there are revolutionary systems which hold that in order to have a right to expect that the Kingdom of God may sooner or later come of its own accord and be visible both in the confines of the church and in political, economic and social relationships, the church has internally merely to give free course to the Holy Spirit and externally merely to let the power of faith and hope which she possesses have free play. Both systems equally overlook the fact that to bridge the gulf between what has already happened and what has not yet become visible is not a task committed to us. And both equally overlook the fact that he who wants to gain peace for himself in this matter can only be a servant of unrest, and conversely that he who wants peace here, may not desire to escape unrest in any direction whatever. Both systems equally overlook the one real bridge which leads across the gulf—the Word of God and faith. It is of this bridge that the Confession reminds us once more when it reminds us of the gift vouchsafed and promised to the church. It reminds us not of any good deeds whether revolutionary or conservative which the church might have to perform, but of the gift which God has vouchsafed and will vouchsafe to the church.

In describing this gift the Confession mentions two things—the *comfort* of sins forgiven and the *hope* of resurrection and eternal life. It mentions these two in particular, clearly in reference to the concluding words of what is called the Apostles' Creed, which forms the secret clue to the whole document. Note however that these two things correspond precisely to the nature of the gulf which runs right through the middle of the church and the life of Christians. Note further how both in their own way indicate the judgement of God and with it the closing of that gulf which is to be accomplished by God and not by us. And note finally how both of them point us to the one real bridge by which alone we can cross the gulf here and now.

The forgiveness of sins is the gift bestowed on us by God, the comfort which we may lay hold of and possess, although our reconciliation with God is still hidden, hidden in what happened on Calvary and not yet visible in what we call our Christian life and not visible either in the historical form of the church or in our political service to God. But even here and now, in the midst of the contradiction of our existence, we are not unreconciled. And why are we not unreconciled ? Because our reconciliation is hidden *there* at what happened on Calvary. And that place there is greater than our present position here. The time of Jesus Christ is more important than our time. And what comforts the church is that our present position is seen in the light of that place and our times are utterly in the hands of Him Who revealed Himself at that time as the Lord. There and then the gulf was already closed for to-day. There the judgement of God has already taken place in so far as His verdict on us has already been given and He has already decided there in our favour with justice and mercy. We are startled by the utter insufficiency of our Christian life and by the fact that the true and false church continue to exist visibly together, and startled too by the dreadful questionableness and danger of our political service of God. We may well be frightened and ought to be. But we have something more pressing to do than to be frightened. We have to accept the comfort that in Jesus Christ there is forgiveness of all the sin with which we could charge ourselves and with which others could charge us, and this without any merit on our part, and yet in accordance with justice and with full validity. The charge against us has been brought already in a more terrible form than we or anyone else could bring it. But also the verdict has already been given and is to the effect that in Jesus Christ we are in the right before God. This is still more important and right, actually it is infinitely more important and right, than the other fact that apart from Jesus Christ we must without any doubt be in the wrong in everything. The more pressing thing which we have to do is to have faith, i.e. to hold firm to the fact that we have been put in the right in Jesus Christ, and in Him alone, but in Him for all time. The more pressing thing which we have to do is to live in this faith at every point, in our personal life, in the church and in the State. In this faith we lay hold of and possess the forgiveness of all our sin, and therefore in this faith we shall live as those who are comforted. This is the gift of comfort which God has given His church.

And now the gift promised us by God is *the resurrection of the body and eternal life*—the hope which we may lay hold of and possess, although our reconciliation with God is still hidden, hidden with Christ in God and thus not visible as yet in any of the spheres we have mentioned. Once again, even here and now, we are not unreconciled. And why are we not unreconciled? The reason is that our reconciliation is hidden, not merely somewhere or other, but there with Christ in God and that thus the time lying before us is in the same hands as that which lies behind us. This is the hope of the church. Jesus Christ alone is her hope, just as Jesus Christ alone is her comfort. We have, strictly speaking, absolutely no knowledge of the resurrection of the body and eternal life beyond what the Word of God tells us, and it tells us that

Jesus Christ has arisen from the dead and lives eternally with God and that His resurrection and eternal life *are* our future also, because He is our Lord, the Lord of Creation and of our whole existence, both our souls and bodies, and because we belong to Him and not to ourselves. But in knowing this we know enough. In Him the verdict on us has been not only given but put into effect. If His righteousness means resurrection from the dead and eternal life and if His righteousness is our righteousness, then what we have to await and what is revealed to us as our future can only be resurrection and eternal life. Such is the hope in which we may live—once more in all spheres, in our personal life, in the church and in the State. All the darkness of our present position is not dark enough to resist such light as this. All our feeling of weakness, all our lack of assurance and the anxiety of which our hearts can be full at the present time, cannot be great enough to destroy the strength and confidence with which we may live in this light. But life in this light is life from and with the Word of God in which the risen Jesus Christ meets us continually. Because He does so, and because He permits His Word continually to be spread abroad and to be heard, our hope cannot die or be thwarted, or degenerate into weariness and despair, but can and will hold its ground in the midst of every kind of weariness and despair. But for this very reason we must continue in faith and in adherence to the Word of God. Any future life other than that of the Word and so of Jesus Christ Himself could only consist in our condemnation and eternal death, of which indeed the Confession also warns us. But this can only be mentioned as a warning, an indication of what man might be if left to himself and thus lost, but what in Jesus Christ he cannot be, a reminder of the fact that outside the Word of God there is no life but only temporal and eternal torment. If we adhere to the Word of God, we can and shall think of this torment, of which the Confession speaks, only as something that has fallen into oblivion for time and eternity.

III

We have come to the end. I promised at the beginning of these lectures to render a service to what is called Natural Theology—to its establishment and propagation—by confronting it with its exact opposite, the teaching of the Reformation, without saying any more about it itself. It has now been so confronted. I believe that there is no important statement in the Scottish Confession and no important statement occurring in my lectures either, which the representative of Natural Theology can avoid considering as the direct opposite of his own tenets and therefore of necessity extraordinarily interesting and profitable for his own particular undertaking. I feel therefore that I have fulfilled my obligations toward the Gifford lectures.

I close with a short observation about *prayer*, with which the Confession ends: " Arise, O Lord, and let thy enemies be confounded ; let them flee from thy presence that hate Thy godlie name. Give thy servands strenth to speake thy word in bauldness, and

let all Natiouns cleave to thy trew knawledge.
Amen."

Its first sentence comes from Psalm 68, 2, the second
sentence from Acts 4, 29, the third seems to be a free
composition on the part of the authors of the Confession.
The teaching of the Reformation is only rightly understood when it is realised that its Confession of faith
must end with prayer and therefore naturally must
begin with prayer too, and that the only prayer possible
at this place must be the one found here, " Arise,
O Lord," and " give Thy servants strength "—the
prayer for God's Word and Revelation, and the prayer
for faith and thus in the first instance and in the second
a prayer for God's own action, which alone makes
amends for what we ourselves shall do badly on all
occasions, however hard we strive after right knowledge
of God and right service of God. The church, by
praying and praying thus, declares that she puts her
trust not in herself but in the comfort and hope, whose
name is Jesus Christ—and in the power of the name
of God the Father, Son and Holy Spirit, the one true
God, to whom alone all Honour and Glory is due.
By praying and praying thus the church declares that
she is crossing the gulf by the one real bridge. Without
prayer of this kind Reformation teaching would have
no real foundation. All its statements, strictly speaking, can only be understood, if one allows oneself to
be called by them to prayer of this kind. Natural
Theology has this advantage over the teaching of the
Reformation that it has no need of prayer of this kind,
and requires neither to begin nor end with it. What it
claims to know about God, the world and man can

most certainly be known without such prayer. Is this an advantage? I wish to leave this question open, after having indicated once more the dimension to which men must turn their gaze if the statements of Reformed Theology are not merely to be heard and discussed, but recognised as the Words of Truth.

INDEX

I. BIBLE QUOTATIONS

II. Names

A

Aaron, 61, 170
Abel, 170
Aberdeen, 164
Abraham, 61
Adam, 42, 46, 47, 49, 61
Amos, 170
Annas, 170
Anti-Christ, 230
Aquinas, Thomas, 20
Augustine, 200

B

Baal, 22, 63
Basel, 164
Bethel, 170
Bethlehem, 78

C

Caiaphas, 63, 170
Cain, 170
Calvary, 28, 52, 78, 84, 86, 236, 239
Calvin, 8, 52, 78 ff.
Canaan, 61
Communists, 168
Corinth, 162

D

David, 61, 65
Denmark, 187
Descartes, 17

E

Easter, 30, 87 ff.
Edinburgh, 164
Egypt, 30, 61, 200
Elijah, 22
England, 187
Ephesus, 162
Eve, 49
Exile, the, 61

F

Feuerbach, Ludwig, 33

G

Gentiles, the, 62
Germany, 187, 226
Gifford, Lord, 3, 243
Goethe, 156
Good Friday, 30

H

Heidelberg Catechism, 99, 118, 138
Henderson, Prof. G. D., 234
Hitler, 226
Hungary, 187

I

Immanuel, 37, 44
Islam, 21
Israel, 30, 60 ff., 65, 151, 196

J

Jahweh Kyrios, 28, 65
Jeremiah, 61, 65
Jerusalem, 170
Jews, 151
Josiah, 225
Judas, 63

K

Knox, John, 10, 229

L

Luther, 8, 91
Lutherans, 79

M

Mary, 135
Messiah, 37, 58, 86, 97, 151, 196
Mohammed, 21
Moses, 61, 65
Mount Carmel, 22

INDEX OF NAMES

72215175R00158

Made in the USA
Columbia, SC
17 June 2017